Rose Is a Verb

Rose Is a Verb

Neo-Georgics

KAREN AN-HWEI LEE

ROSE IS A VERB
Neo-Georgics

Slant
An Imprint of Wipf and Stock Publishers
199 W. 8th Ave., Suite 3
Eugene, OR 97401

www.wipfandstock.com

HARDCOVER ISBN: 978-1-7252-7595-9
PAPERBACK ISBN: 978-1-7252-7594-2
EBOOK ISBN: 978-1-7252-7596-6

Cataloguing-in-Publication data:

Names: Lee, Karen An-hwei.
Title: Rose is a verb : neo-Georgics / Karen An-hwei Lee.
Description: Eugene, OR: Slant, 2021
Identifiers: ISBN 978-1-7252-7595-9 (hardcover) |ISBN 978-1-7252-7594-2 (paperback) | ISBN 978-1-7252-7596-6 (ebook)
Subjects: LCSH: Agriculture — Poetry | Pastoral poetry | Nature — Poetry. | American poetry — 21st century.
Classification: PS3612.E3435 R674 2021 (paperback) | PS3612.E3435 (ebook)

07/08/21

Georgic:
A poem or book dealing with agricultural or rural topics.
—*Oxford Dictionaries*

For you shall eat the fruit of your hands:
happy shall you be, and it shall be well with you.
—*Psalm 128:2*

The time for harvest, the time for planting seeds,
The time to brave the unfaithful sea with oars,
The time to bring the warboats down to water,
The time to fell the pines. . . .
—First *Georgic* by Virgil

Virgil's call to himself to "rise" at the end of the *Eclogues* (10.75 sur-
gamus) was answered by a rise in generic level with his next work,
the *Georgics*. . . . As with the *De rerum natura* [*On the Nature of Things*, by
Lucretius], the central concern is rather the place in the world of human
beings and the possibilities of happiness.
—*Oxford Classical Dictionary*

Hold onto what is good,
even if it's a handful of earth.
Hold onto what you believe,
Even if it's a tree that stands by itself.

Hold onto what you must do,
Even if it's a long way from here.
Hold onto your life,
Even if it's easier to let go.

Hold onto my hand,
Even if I've gone away from you.

—Pueblo Indian Prayer

CONTENTS

PROEMIUM: TWELVE QUESTIONS FOR SAGES AND STRANGERS

Farolitos glow in the adobe curve of a hill—
I pose a dozen questions to strangers.

1. What is your love-offering today?
2. What or who bears the light?
3. What was not otherwise yesterday?
4. What do you hold onto, even if it _____?
5. What ordinary miracles arose today?
6. Who are the antennae in your life?
7. What cliff does prayer mount in your soul?
8. Where are signs of divine vs. human creation?
9. Which of the ordained days have you lived?
10. What heart-questions are unaddressed?
11. What is your conversation with God?
12. What gift do you send into the world?

In a turn of fate, or a gesture of telos—
        of the teleological, a sign or goal—a man
                brushes my sleeve at the airport
with an inquiry. When was the last time
you were deliriously happy?

The sage asks, why does it matter?
    Who says we ought to pursue happiness?
    Why not? asks a stranger.

I.

On Love in Millennial Weather

GOLD-BLACK CADENZA OF NOONS

Nanograms of rose-plumed bullion
towed onto furred heads of pollen,
frenzy shot through salvos of gold,
wingspeed over wingspan—
A bee's mass far exceeds its airfoil,
yet its speed verbs a heliotrope's ear,
humming, I rose, I rose, I rose.
The sage asks, is labor a miracle
or levitation of the mundane?
Oyster-moss, gold-black cadenza
of noons, of brassy squash blossoms
loaded with pollen cargo, powdered
queens of unbleached wax, of honey
royalactin. Never smoked or drank,
fondness of calla lilies with napes
of neon trailing to a sea—
Yes, kissing astro-silk—*taraxacum*—
kindness stroked out of milkweed,
epidemics, fruit-bat fever.
Do no harm.

ECLOGUES WITH STRANGERS

Yield of sister ice-blossoms, of apiarian labor,
double-edged nectar of eclogues. Is a lyric cut
of a mytho-siren's tongue? Is happiness
restrained by jute-cords?

ROSE-SPILLED JUG OF PRAISE

Orbed sea-petals of global indigo unfurl their veils,
rain commingles with oaky wine notes, a ferrous
floral carbon, floral iron: corpus of sage-blossom,
not envy-laden venom. Do not shun firelight's
greenheart candor sipping your apiarian wax,
                              a rose-spilled jug of praise.
Waterless sink-basin on the moon, *sea of crisis*—
ashtray of lunar basalt and shelled pistachios
used to aid memory. No happiness. Not yet.
Citronella tears in the hazelwood hair of a girl
with burned eyelashes. Yes, say every name.
Davina. Elidad. Jacynth. Kayla. Luvena.
Prayers bless our lobes of wax. Olives purr
in oiled tongues of flame: jacaranda, myrtle,
African tulip, names of flame trees: illawarra,
firebush, royal, and flame-in-the-woods. Yes,
yes, all the girl's names translate as *beloved.*
Bugonia is not ultimately about bees alone.
Praise, neither tangible nor bodiless offering—
an adobe dove with a clay shovel for a heart,
neither flesh of bird, fish, nor reptile—a rose.

SOLAR VALVE OF LOVE, SEA WALL

Neither nymph nor cloud of the troposphere,
I dozed at an altitude of forty-thousand feet
above sea level, I saw mothers in a lighthouse
with their children: orchid-haired great-aunts
called by name to a helical stair. *Young woman*
but not *young mother.* All the young women,
half-sprouted females with grasshopper shins,
were asked to stand in a circle. Spiral cupola,
neweled staircase in a lighthouse room of ships,
I do not belong anywhere. Not young mothers,
not even half-grown women, dayspring girls,
not our grandmothers whose bodies exploded
to give light to generations. A flash unseals
alabaster vases, a decolonized female dagger,
a lightning rod, a solar valve of love, sea wall,
a cloud of grasshoppers-to-locusts in famine,
a chimeric hive of honeybees on a turntable
singing the waxy heat of a groove on a gallery
deck in ruthless weather, hailstones pelting
ocean icicles, a hybrid of ice and barnacle
or brine and icicle, *brinicles.*

DELIRIOUS PLAZAS OF STAR DUST

Defamations of love in millennial weather—
Genetically, we're delirious plazas of star dust.
Ad astra per aspera, to the stars via adversity,
                          of fevered nucleosynthesis
fusing hydrogen to helium in stellar plasma,
beryllium and carbon, kilos of neutrino ash
mined in our hymning flesh, zocalo of suns.

In a seaside villa of seraphim, baths, gardens,
God strums a rain-guitar while an ebony flame
                          swirls over lingering questions—
Who said we are entitled to happiness,
asks the sage. Stop slandering love,
says the stranger. Stop ruining things.
Whose happiness, whose ecstasy,
replies the sage.

Not delirious. Not the moon. Not flamenco,
rather, *flame.* Metronome of an aural pulse
on a crime index of one versus a hundred
in the firehills. *Our safest refuge is Christ,*
says blindness, a girl opening the shutters
to the stars while closing her eyes at night.

LASIANDRA

Nocturnal dialogues of a diurnal soothsayer—
Lasiandra, trellised violet ivy not yet pruned
in a rain of distilled spirits. I am older than daylight.

The daylight says, *false.*
Older than you, and the word is older than both of us,
wildfire of phthalo irises, our witness.

Rephrase a question raptured on cloud nine—
When did you last experience
a racing heart, tachycardia—or trace of fever?

MOTTLED SADNESS OF ICEWINE

Not in this world, blooming violet says
on its axis of rotation, translation of a body
on a revolution of axial precession
over the centuries, four thousand years,
of silver iodide in a hundred rockets
seeding rainclouds over a city outside Beijing.
Slurry of moonlight bleeds
on a heat-dulled blade of garden shears
gas-torched to denature viruses fatal
to *Phalaenopsis* orchids.

Sad mottled light
of muscatel floods our winter vineyards,
a valley of peach-colored glass
caramelized wherever *dulce de leche*
etherizes woe or no ether at all
as a figurative solvent for regret.
O, we are literally plazas of star dust,
carbon, hydrogen, oxygen, sulfur—
spinning clouds of anonymity.
Estamos literalmente
plazas de polvo de estrellas.
Ash to ash.

RESURRECTIONS IN MONOCHROME

After I turned forty, a bit older than the age Jesus
walked on water, I paid a sum of forty-one cents
to ride a bus across featureless roads to the sea.
Forty-one cents for every year of life, no minor
jubilee for a small-boned soul seeking miracles
in everyday monochrome. *Everyday. Miracles.*
Is this an oxymoron, or meager ingratitude?
A pastor once described our journey as *a long
obedience in the same direction.* Disembarked
at the station with seagulls diving overhead
crying to savor the fishbone ghosts of tilapia
after the inland sea was choked by salts.

A confession. In a dream, I stayed inside.
No nymph, starlet, nor queen bee, no diva
fated to eat jelly, to lay royal eggs on wax
for the rest of mortality. No, I was born
a little human being, one who hoarded
forty-one cents of tooth cash eons ago,
fourteen bits of sea glass, mermaid's tears
recycled out of the world's broken bottles—
a formula for tiny obsessions by the hour.
Fallen paradise is no subset of happiness
or vice versa, no superset of equilibrium—
mediocre lust, overlapping with ecstasy's
euphoric element, is common to all sets—
ergo, no vexation exists in this sum,
minus your envy for the fog
on this rogue biomass heating
nearly half a degree
per century.

IF A STRANGER SAYS

And on your journey through the grove of years,
if a stranger says to you—

How do you feel about the wars we fought in _____?
When did you come here?

May I touch your dusty, unbrushed hair?
Where are you going?

Say a phrase in _____ language.
When was the last time you felt *non compos mentis*?

Neither sane nor in your right mind, I mean?
And what saith the atoms
in this starry grove of ash?

GRAVITY OF BLACK-FRUITING CULTIVARS

Gravity of black-fruiting cultivars in a grove, fat drupes
crushed by millstone. Pomaced blood arose, oil bottled
as a gift—unskinned, pulped olives, fruit-picking bags,
batiste summer frocks wreathed in sage-colored leaves.
Radishes in milk, not cream. Quinoa and mizuna greens,
parsley sprigs with zest. The feckless amethyst of wisteria,
angelica-stained ears of zygos, of glazed bundt spice-cakes.
Of wild boar thinning while the quail and peahens fatten.
Boiled orange peel and cinnamon bark, a slim girl afire.
Fougasse aux olives wrapped in yards of toile, perfumed
love-gifts, *charismata*—prophetic, electrostatic, pyretic
alchemy of pheromones, aromatic covalency of ketones
and aldehydes, of fruity esters and sparkling alcohols,
ecstatic yoking of molecular oxygen. *Now. Breathe.*
Molecular biologists freely loan their songs of order
to poets, marveling at *ecstatic* and *electrostatic*
in a breath, the vestal names of cloudscapes,
mutability thinned to a vapor—cirrus, anvil,
lenticular, cumulonimbus, altostratus, rain.

MIRACLES OF ORIGIN, DEGREE, OR SEQUENCE

On the hydrophilic nature of orchids, generated
by lace-cut doves of the Holy Spirit or *Spiritus
Sanctus,* snowflakes irresistibly drawn to yes
and yes, water to water, monergism by grace.
Is this how the invisible makes itself visible?
For categories of miracles, Aquinas lists three.
First, origin or nothing to thingness, the birth
of Christ. Secondly, of degree—quantitative
magnitude like a boy's meal feeding a hungry
multitude with fishes and loaves. Thirdly,
of sequence beyond usual events of normal
causation, such as the dead raised to life.

NOT A HAND-ROSE. VERB. NOT A ROSE

A cloud the size of a hand rose above the sea
at a distance, followed by rain. On miracles,
the first one occurs in terms of degree or level,
as in multiplied fishes and loaves. The second,
a miracle of time sequence outside a given order
of natural operations, i.e., resurrecting the dead
or delaying twilight by half a day on a battlefield.
The final type manifests in a normative sequence
without natural origin, for example, a little cloud
the size of a hand rose above the sea after a man
prayed for rain. *Not a hand-rose. Verb. Not a rose.*
The prophet was a man like us, says the apostle.
A confession: I am worried about my lassitude
in this regard. Outside salvation, other miracles
signal us as living vessels of divine love. *Why*
does not render me a skeptic, yet I briefly forgo
pomegranate black chai: abnegation of desire,
a love-offering. Or is this deed superfluous
in light of salvation, the supreme miracle?
Fasting is a negation of desire: or desire
is rendered transparent: one confesses,
      yields a soul: zero rose.
Cross the marked flesh.
Selah.

RADIOGRAPH WITH WINGS IN TUMULT

No cessationist, I do not believe miracles ceased
with first-century apostles. Yet in girlhood,
I doubted. Now I wonder if this blindness
to miracles other than salvation masqueraded
as mere ingratitude, so lackluster.

And the last time you were deliriously happy?
This question from a stranger is a distraction,
apple cider clouded by mother-of-vinegar—
neither water nor wine but a mass of rod-shaped
prokaryotes metabolizing wine to vinegar.

Redirect the question.
Forget delirium. When was the last time you were happy?
Did you say, *delphinium?*

OTHER DISEQUILIBRIUM

Zika, not a girl's name.
Ebola, not a blossom.
Not phlox, digitalis or foxglove, calendula
gold in its zygote. Or other disequilibrium
of resounding bluebells—
Cost of *forever*, only forty-one cents,
years to this day. How far are you able
to journey alone into a wasteland?
Count the cost, says the stranger.

On beauty as fever chills,
an oxymoron. Indigo batik
of stars, black lilies, or tears,
of bliss in negative,
asphyxiation or other
disequilibrium
strolling through
this insufferable grove
of sunstroke triggered
by climate change.

Prayer is not a radiograph
of x-rayed wings
or a cylinder of nitrous oxide
bursting in a surgical suite,
the last firestorm.
Weft of calendared silk,
mordant dye unraveled on a bolt
unpinned, let go. Or a midnight
saguaro like a ghost ship.
Prayer is none of these,
says the sage.

ONES WHO INVITE YOU TO GO SWIMMING

Why rarely women, always men,
ask those questions. No formal address,
no sequence of normative gestures
preceding a comical query—
Is chocolate an anti-depressant?
Do you feel melancholy? Why?
Do you want children? Why not?

No in Mandarin and Spanish to those
who invite you to go swimming, braid your hair,
hold your hand, fill your pail with nickels—
yes, little girl—or take you for a ride. *Say no.*
Pay for a bus ride to the Salton Sea
where gulls circled overhead in wavering heat,
a mirage soaking in more conviction
than reality itself, rimming our souls
with a cloud of misericordia,
blessed mercy.

Whether I decline prosaicisms
or not: *Happiness is your choice.*
Nope, it arises from serotonin.
Oxytocin. Dopamine. Endorphins.
Happiness is not an end.
Shun perfectionism. Pray for an hour.
Eating phenylethamine in cacao nibs
keeps no records of wrongs,
more blessedly gives than receives
the yield of an altruistic life
beyond pharmacodynamics. Love
unconditionally, yes.

ROSEFIRE IN UNTILLED HEAT

On letting go, on forgiveness. On holding or not.
Rosefire in the untilled heat of August rushes the sill,
yet I cannot touch the apex of love in haste.

                              Affliction, contentment, even bliss?
                              Yes, dear rosefire of untilled heat—
                    A prayer warrior dyes her beehive hair
                              autumnal fire, cinnamon rouge,
                                        all the rage lately.

Tossing, turning in a hot borax night,
who is so angry? Is it you?
Did a beloved stranger in a lost universe
crush your heart in summed algebraic
shards, plotting a heart's coordinates
on polar axes drawn on lines of credit,
          our debt of love to one another?
Whose heart was it? Was it infarction
or infatuation, a bitter taste of inedible

                              rupture, of bleeding
                         in a cracked rib of light,
                    of bones weeping hopelessness
                         in a rush of sloping roses?

FLESH-DOME WITH THE LEVITY OF BIRDS

Hold onto ones who love, even their saline
dreams of brackish water in coralline quarts,
of winter leaning on blackthorn canes.
This one, who forsook carousing
at midnight, tilts her middle years
on a lazy susan of wet velvet cake,
birds flying with a will to love
and let live—a woman's cast-off mates
sink one by one into the soil, heavy
and moist as black forest gâteau.
Whose body is spinning on this earth?
A cross with a *corpus* is a crucifix.
A crucifix without a *corpus* is a cross.
Hold onto ones whom you love:
What does a *corpse* have to do with this?
Rose is a body, rose is a *corpus*,
and rose is a verb—
What is your bread of fellowship?
You and a loved one? A stranger?
The body itself, a flesh-dome
with the levity of birds?

SOUGHT ON A FLIGHT OF HAPPINESS

More than strangers in the noise of whiteness—
lovebirds, male and female, on a flight to a north
shore of a cilantro-sprigged sea—
                    a man dropped his boarding pass
while storing his guitar overhead.
Yes, this was back in the day of paper passes.
He gestured to seat B. *Put it over there. Over.*
No *would you please.* Or *thank you.* Lovebird,
a bluish, thin-boned woman younger than me,
sat in seat A. Blue-eyed petite on his shoulder,
bird-arms clasping his torso for the long flight,
she gazed out an oval window without a word,
settling in a nest of sleep, drowsy ring of heat
coupled over a great lake's sky, more inner sea,
lesser blue. Her name was indeed a bird's,
the flycatcher, *phoebe.*

Light, she gasped, *the light breaking over there.*
Navy majorelle pea-coat, a faux moissanite clasp,
ash-blonde hair. Sleepily, she murmured, *women
who work on planes dress like clouds.* Pupils
flash in stellar light: the eyes look right through,
ones my Fujian forebears said, *blank* or *ghostly.*
Film negative, *not there.* Minimalist, stark realism
in smoldering flares of dialogue, ennui in the third
person, flash fiction without quotation marks
at 24,000 feet, a place where I finally glimpse
why minimalism.

As the airplane descended,
the man gazed without seeing an Asian woman
on the aisle seat who said nothing for the duration

of the flight, partaking without his permission
an insular space with his beloved.
Was this the stranger who asked a question?
I reflect, *we are only loaned to our loved ones.*
Hold everyone you love

                         loosely, my love.

QUESTIONS IN THE SHAPES OF ROAN HORSES

The sage asks, *how many times*
must we pray until the wind moves?

The wind says, *until the sage*
ceases asking the question.

The sage asks, *how do we know*
when the response has arrived?

The wind says, *when the answer*
holds the question.

Prayer is a salt-beaten stormwrack of driftwood
lying in the shapes of roan horses on a shore —
fashioned as ornamental lamps for a fireplace,
a mangrove root lovingly varnished for a lintel,
a pneumatophore lashed by an ocean squall,
a rack of sequoia in copper-stippled light,
a legible testimony to grace underwater
over a thousand *thousand* times, yes.
To live. To breathe. Underwater.

Once, at minimum.

ON COLOR THEORY IN VOIRE DIRE

After a draught of whiteness and xenophobia,
a brusque chill of strangers in the troposphere,
I serve my civic duty. *Voir dire* in a courthouse,
fountain trees droop in a hysteria of hate,
violence. Stand-your-ground. Please see
olive shoulders outside whiteness, flint-eyed.
See our true skinnedness. Breathe a cloud
of non-white noise. *She. Is. The only. Olive.*
Girl. In the box. See *race*, not a shadow of doubt,
                    of manslaughter blossoming
        in shades of riot gear, of tear gas. *Do you see*
when you look? Pardon me, wilderness
for seeing
for saying—

I am an olive tree with the shoulders of a girl.
Who, I say, using a soft pronoun, not verb.
Our defendant sitting over there. Black, white.
Brown or black. This is not a grammar exercise.
Who or whom. Look at me. *A woman. Of color.*
Here. Please use prayer to heal people with love
in these end-times of fire and ice. *Over here.*

SUFFERED IN THE FLESH, ROSE-COLORED

Hold onto our season of toil and bone, of kith and kin
rattled by Santa Ana foehn winds gusting thru arroyos
at no price to you. *Hold on, let go.* Hold onto the heights
even if you lack the force to grip sheer rockface, if you fail
to see your prayers move mountains, or if a blasted, ragged
road is a bleached flag on your spine. Rose is a verb
which has arisen, or a hope made fragrant by holiness—
God also suffered in the flesh: rose-colored, impaled
and lacerated, bone-deep on a hill. *Hold on, let go.*
        No one has asked me to apostatize, not yet. Never.
Most of us may live in quiet desperation. Most of us
do not live as daily martyrs who crucify *yes* to ignoble
flesh. A soul torn by fish-bones plucked out of skin
holds onto this rack of driftwood, a littoral sea-gift
for our tinted glass bottles of seasoning except sage.
Wild black sage in the fog, out of sight this evening
when we seasoned an old baguette for onion ribollita.
The habit of prayer seasons without a book or a body,
without instructions, only spindles of wisdom spinning
every hour. Girls of all races over the globe—brutalized
in the crosshairs of proxy wars—pray to God, pleading
for their bodies. Souls. *Please listen.* Now is the time
to listen. *Please listen.* Listen, says the sage.

FRAGRANCE OF UNBOTTLED TEARS

As the sea rose, hypothermia set in.
Moaning with the waves, delirious men hung
while a neap tide rose.

> At sixteen, I read this novel without seeing the irony
> or incarnation. *Silence* did not drive me away.

Martyrs were lashed to masts at low tide.
On the contrary, drawn to pure flame,
I was reborn years later.

ECHELONS OF GRACE AS INHERITANCE

Faceless star, attar of roses
in a divine factory of burnt offerings
fixed my attention.

Oddly, contrary to my recollection,
martyrs hung upside-down and bled
over pits, not tied to masts at low tide.

Salvation is not without a face. A mystery.

I am the light of the world.
Where are you, my love?

PRAYER AS SHOT-GLASSES OF DAYLIGHT BLOSSOMING

Some of us do not live as strangers. Sages of resilience,
hold on, then let go. Prayer sings a lightning rod of grace,
grounded yet blood-soaked. Praise the chitin-filtered air
in spiracles of insects, feathered book-lungs, deliquescent
respiration in scorpions radiolucent as x-rayed diamonds,
air-breathing spiders or crickets, ruddy cardinal spinach
raised by pacifist vegan scribes. Ethylene of stone fruit,
hormones of non-genetically modified endocarp, pods.
In our fallenness, we fix our attention on God who is
a thousand-thousand shot-glasses of aromatic daylight
soaked in neroli-bergamot perfume, linalool of modern
spikenard. A thousand aromas in fourteen-carat vials
of electroplated platinum, rose oil, orris root, clove buds,
tinctures of frankincense and myrrh, ylang ylang, a rack
of wedding gowns in the cool, damask for the banquets
as evening katydids quake in foliate spires of aspens—
would you say this is worth a year's wages? What right
do we have to this expenditure? What of white women
bewailing a predisposition to melanoma in the presence
of other diseases, of *lightness* per *whiteness?* Does this
imply women of color are the sun? Yes, of course, yes.

ALGEBRAIC SHARDS OF A GLASSY HEART

Rutilance of praise,
                    of fish blood or jubilation,
        rubies not *rue*.
The sage says: write this a thousand times.
I desire nothing. I desire nothing. I desire
nothing. Fracturing of algebraic shards,
a glassy heart. Algebra red as a bolero
of slow-tempo fires in hurricane lamps.
Confession. In a chandelier ballroom,
I speak bold untruths—
I desire nothing. I desire nothing.
        Blessing in disguise. *Immune to envy.*
In this millennium, angels witness
        how we inadvertently revive measles
by weighing the hazards of vaccination
                against the risk of infection,
no longer immune to annihilation
                    by an abundance of caution,
    desiring nothing in the end.
Is this true, I ask with rue.

LISTEN, SILENT AS ANAGRAMS OF ONE ANOTHER

White woman asks, *are you truly forty-one years old?*
She looks down. *May I see your identification, miss?*
O, such queries are rather amiss. Flowering in reverse,
a creek of black grass, as maidenhair, ginkgo biloba—
a fountain of ages reverse-engineered, the water of life
flowing backwards. *Fons vitae, aquae vitae,*
river stones as mute satellites tuned to God, woman
who is ageless. Say *listen* and *silent* are anagrams.
Readings of annular rings in a jurassic metasequoia
listen for fourteen, forty-one, or four hundred years
in my infinite torso, says the father of the universe,
the alpha and omega. Do you remember the flood?
Prayer as fauna predating fabulously winged insects
aligned to a magnetic field, southing quietly, divining
a geomagnetic reversal once every ten thousand years
whether we witness the shifts or not, whether or not
butterflies are evolving or not, whether this is truly
a young earth or old earth bedded in a toile
of bridal mists whirling in solar darkness.

VIA NEGATIVA

God is now here. No where. No here. Or nowhere.
To say who God is
by saying who God is not,
via negativa. On prayer as a roped-off room where love
holds you by the bones until you calm down. Praying
by rose-velvet drapes or the silkiest synthetic mohair
so there is no harm to angora goats. *Am a God of war.*
Am not a God of war.

You are not beautiful. You are beautiful.
Wear my antithesis of beauty
in a box of negative space,
of genetic predisposition
or mutagenesis, a surprise.
You are beautiful, says the stranger.
And who is beauty? replies the sage.

PRAYER AS VERMILION ROSE-HIPS ON FIRE

Strangers adrift on the bayside said *angel*
while sages said nothing on the city subway.
Two decades ago, when I moved to this coast,
I stacked my books in a room without shelves.
As I stood on a chair, the bay's gray margin
breathed a soft roof of clouds at the skyline—
for years, I lived as an angel in a leaden wall.
Summer, the books lightened with the clarity
of moth's wings, no longer elemental tongues
of those no longer alive.

On intercession as forked lightning
in the blazing retinas of fishermen:
retinas not *retsinas,* pine-resin wine.
On prayer as undersea minefields on fire
like fuel tanks of blistered vermilion roses
or a region of blindness riddled by war.
A province of dyspathy fraught with soul
damage fights battles within its borders,
lesions in a retrograde menstrual tide
ebbing and flowing with bodily strife,
a ruby nation-state of endometriosis.

LOVE AS A GINGER-FLAVORED BALM

On love as a ginger-flavored balm for our heartshot wounds,
fiery spice of *jiang*. Or love as *kairos*-breathed sustenance.
On asking for a javelin when my blood rises to a glass ceiling.
On why I see red flags in the air if white xenophobia rejects
racial reconciliation. Often means, to our backs, *we still
do not wish to see you but will tolerate your presence.*
Often means, to our faces, *in your anger, do not sin.*
Translates to a string of obscenities, not love or equity.
Let us not settle for tolerance when we could love
and be loved. Dear xenophobia: hold all you love
so loosely—
                    loosely, my love.

II.

On the Beauty of Modified Fruitage

SHIELDING A GIRL, HER DYNAMITE TOPAZ SOUL

Shield a girl from an exploding grenade—
topaz does not melt, immune to dynamite.

On fever in adiabatic transfer of work as energy
heated to flash point.

Santa Anas out of a high desert, a fever—
dwarf-willow arroyos and vales swept to the sea.

Wake in the night, disoriented—
wind-thrashed eucalyptus.

Which saint do I miss, Santa Ana or Santa Fe,
the coastal mesa or sagebrush steppes?

Gift of healing, one of the *charismata*
of *Spiritus Sanctus,* kisses the flatlands.

On warning seabirds of electric storms—
is this a form of cormorant's prayer?

How do we send a love-offering?
Which of the ordained days are we in now?

BLAZING HONEY IN FOUR LANGUAGES

Nine noons I awaited
a cherrywood harp, *alabazana*—
river birch sound-box, lemon-oiled,
glowing on chamois folded by a luthier's
angel lying on her side in a mirror-box
shouldered by a courier. Afar, brushfires
fizzled after rainfall. Is happiness
a pear in a compote of melancholy,
a rain-rutted road to girlhood lessons,
a rust-colored brook reeking of gasoline fumes,
a gypsy moth fanning a Japanese architect's
fish-shaped house with a porthole
for the eye, a cherrywood tree
hand-split, planed, buffed for praise?

Happiness mixes *blancmange*
out of a carrageenan sky over lacquered persimmon,
Santa Lucia fir, magenta crape-myrtle,
silver dollars of a eucalyptus vaporized by liquid sun,
a magnesium torch flaming thousands of degrees
underwater, cattleya orchid of blanched fire,
a botanical monograph of floral cyanotypes,
silver bromide at one end of the room
or a hand-strung zither on the other.

Brushfires fizzle eleven miles away
as a girl spells *honey* in four languages—
miel, fengmi, hachimitsu, mật ong.
Tongued verbal sweetness
of envoweled quartos,
quartets of consonance,
of quatrains.

ON PRAYER, AN ECLIPSE OF MOTHS

Jade-veined luna without a tongue or proboscis,
fated to die of starvation, emerges from her pupal
and instar stages to the adult imago with day-old
celadon wings. *A group of moths is an eclipse.*
A moth spreads on a summer screen, rear kitchen
where a steaming dish of saffron rice bore the heat
of golden sulfite raisins, almonds, oxidizing flesh
of dark aubergines in a roux of butter and flour.
A group of butterflies is a kaleidoscope. I fail
to set aside the silver for a mug of dove's dung
in a season of war, *five shekels,* whether or not
this was actual dove's dung or a wild vegetable.
I live as a single woman in a time long prior
to the naming of groups of birds, as follows.
*A group of ravens is an unkindness. A group
of swans is a bevy in flight. In turn, a bevy
of flamingos is a flamboyance.*
Neo-georgic echoed by a girl who hears *crepuscular*
yet utters *muscular* then *marsupial* and *corpuscle*
more kith and kin with fauna than flora in genera
or *crepusculum,* the dusk—origami of paper plums
and a *washi* of mulberry paper, six-cornered light.
If we wish to complain of hunger, reflect on this—
a luna moth, at maturity, has no mouth.

A THOUSAND FLORETS OF INBORN ZEAL

North, north, in a compass as if obliterating a code
of fugitive moths in global warming, a red garland
of light-lassoing bougainvillea says, *owe the light
four zeroes of perfume.* Praise lingers on a bright
forehead, a gardener—evening, it bore a late glare
even as his eyes dimmed. Psalm of mission stucco,
skyward carbonate marl closer kin to sea-coral rag
than ichnofossil trace. Saying *ethereal* is too easy,
nor lowly enough. To say it bears the light is good.
*If I abandon my body to flames, yet have not love,
I am nothing.* Gutted truth in bone-dry samaras,
fissured green bearing thousands of flowers no less
haloed in skin than yours, dew-armed rosebushes
who know nothing of georgic catalogues of trees
breathing God at two in the morning, a thousand
florets of inborn zeal shouting in the moonlight—
slow-maturing olive, pliant osier, bending broom,
pear-tree transforming the engrafted apple yield,
perfumed balsams, mountain-ash, yew.

ON PRAYER AS DIALOGUE, ONE OF LISTENING

In the sea fog, dolphins rise in a lagoon of bad weather,
freed at the last minute by a fleet of angels in the cove,
sleigh of flying rivers in carbon-dioxide and methane.
Why does this millennium harm our dolphins, beluga,
daughters of seahorses, the green orphans of crisis?
Forced blood donations. Organ theft. Kidnappings.
Ransoms. *Do not say arrangement. Forced. Rope.*
Did you say, rope? No, I said rape. Rope, rope? No.
Do you know whether this is a valid record of witness
or hot rooibus you drank before you lay down to sleep?
Were you awake? Were you in an altered mind state?
How could you sleep while women burned in cages?
While abandoned children perished in plywood boxes?
What helps you feel safe? Can you remember or tell—
Where are the divine vectors of our avenging arrows?
No more soporific or mythological than feathers shot
off arches of the moon's unfolded wingspan. *Please.*
Shedding tales of slain flesh, calyx on calyx. *Listen.*
Even the strongest of our tendons, ligaments, arteries,
the density of *locus coeruleus,* navy-blue neuromelanin
for dreaming, waking, memory, attention, for kinetoscopic
darkling consciousness, none are adequate vectors alone
to salvation. *Please listen.*

IS THE SOUL NOT A RED GERANIUM

Open fingers camouflaged with pequin chili
as if spoken by the fever-blood of paradise—
No bleeding in paradise. No fever. You turn.
Why should anyone desire delirium at all?
Do you speak Spanish, he says. *Poquito?*
Clouds of pestle-ground chili at *el santuario*
sifted generation to generation on his hands
now unfastening a bag under the counter—
pray he does not ask you to taste it out
of his hand, his finger, his ear, his tongue.
Loitering as if he desires more than this.

What is your dialogue with God
on happiness? On grace while gardening?
Blood-gravity on a vine. *Nightshade blood*
pulses in reverse direction out of a heart,
piquant blood of a transgenic *jaune flamme*
tomato out of aerating lungs, mine-sweeping
or salvaging a wreck, *rapture of the deep*
exposing a crucifix on the miraculous site
of *el pocito*, little dirt well, holy mouth
in mud-brick earth. A bleeding woman
said, let me grab a fistful of this holy dirt
and rub its grit on my afflictions—
renamed as my wandering affections
for chocolate, for dysmenorrhea.
Tierra bendita, a dirt-blessing for illness,
for labor pains of childbirth. Unrequited
no longer. Your durable heart-engine,
marbled toil of muscle, sore revolutions
of a subterranean heart, core of affliction,
says *miracule* as a portmanteau of miracle

and miniscule. Miracule, miracule. *Selah.*

Is the soul not a red geranium?
Rooted in all weather, red and bitter
yet sweet to the bee's eye.
Can it walk on live coals? Why not?
Is attraction no less than chemistries
of procreation? Oxytocin, serotonin,
and endorphins? Firelight of atoms
bound as desire's oxidizing fruitage
or vice versa?

BEJEWELED RADII

Quickened, I rose at daybreak. Arose.
Not peace but serotonin, not worship
or praise but oxytocin, nerve signals
in tissue biopsied with fine needle
aspiration. *Life is more than food,*
and the body more than raiment.

> *Yes and yes.* Fruit yield of rebirth
> as a love-offering, as a shepherd-harpist
> serving as the warrior-king. *Yes and yes.*
> Sacred water, equivalent to those lives
> risked to obtain it.

Is this happiness?
Out of love to love,
it originates from
and returns to God,
bejeweled radii—
alpha and omega.

WILL PRAYER HEAL YOUR BODILY AFFLICTION WITH SPIRITUAL BREAD?

On mosses of post-lyric for a georgic ear,
or lying in more margins than one.

On gratification—
Do not sell your birthright for a mug of pottage.

Hunger hums a bilious melody,
no wafers of fireweed honey

in domed mouths of ovens,
no pressed figs cakes.

CRY OF DOVES, A GIRL FALLING

Cry of doves, a girl falling
in love out of a second-story window
at the sight of a fruitseller's son—
this is my hair, lowered for you,
this is my body, broken for you,
no sin offering of two doves every year.
No tithe in mint and cumin or firstfruits.
How much were two doves in a cage worth?
Alive or not, male or female?
Tragic doves, often said to mate for life,
trussed up in a rucksack.
God is not sleeping. God is not sleeping.
Non est Deus dormientes.
Praying in brusque yet plush darkness,
resinous waist-brushing hair in commas
of fish-tails, of winter swallows. *Pause.*
Diapause, I mean, a form of hibernation
or vice versa. Or the anguish of a stranger
who asks, when was the last time
you were delirious?
God is awake.

MIDNIGHT POISED ON ADOBE SHOULDERS

In essence, an unleavened prologue to hunger—
absence-as-presence or flesh-to-bread-as-body,
figurative transformation or spiritual allegory
in cast-iron molds of round, coin-sized wafers,
capiz-thin as windchimes over a bare sea snail,
as windowpane oysters, lesser sisters of pearl,
a hundred carp scales of fresh lacquer shining
while midnight, poised on adobe-shouldered
arroyos of rosemary and sagebrush, murmurs
in throats of coyotes, hums *la luz, la luz, la luz*
in a running wilderness. The sage asks, where
do angels go in a time of war? Stranger says,
only the angels of death and angels of famine
work in our multitudes. The stranger adds,
why does the sage pose so many questions
without replies? Don't sages give answers?
The sage says, don't you know? Isn't it true
that questions beget more insights about truth?
The stranger replies, and tell me, what is true?
The sage says, here are responses to some queries
you've posed in the past. Do you remember at all?
A widow mourned her girls. A funeral train did not
return us to those we loved most in life, lost hours
not bartered for osier-willow baskets or anything
under the sun, not a valencia orange for radishes
or vice versa. One is not the other. *An eye for an eye,*
as the saying goes, *leaves the whole world blind.*
Retribution is not always just. Revenge in disguise.
Neither is love. Regrets arose in monoxide as she lay
in half-delirium. Why is it called a grandfather clock,
not a grandmother or great-aunt clock? If God
were a woman, she might turn back time

on behalf of my lost girls. The stranger says,
what was the question? The sage says,
do you remember?

OR WHAT IS A HARMONIC MEAN OF LIGHT

Black mission figs without rust-colored fungus in a rainstorm.
Square root of differences between data points and the mean.
Root of variations in hue, flesh texture, tolerance for bruising.

This is standard deviation, said the woman, an ornithologist,
prevernal spring in full force, pear-colored snow blossoming
on zoysia under this mantle. Black mission figs are not black.

What is the standard deviation of light, June to June,
solstice of the longest day? Blackness is not literally black,
blackness dazzling on black is not black.

Hold onto a drop of rooibus as a tonic for perimenopause.
Hold onto a murmur, even if your valves do not seal.
Hold onto your summer love, June to June.

Coral-hued eosin dye or nuclei blue, gram-positive crystal violet.
There is no such thing as immunity to light. Hold a trichrome dye
or triple-colored histology stain even if a dye is a sound,
not a color. *Of innocence, not harm.*

Who knew this tisane would be richer
than red wine, blood-vault of cherries, figs,
and gallic tannin, than erythropoiesis itself?

HYMN OF A BLACK CALYX IN THE MOUTH

Emerald firelight in a rush of flames—
If you stay angry, even your eyelashes will ignite
in the shadow of lion-colored butterflies. Nacre
        of fish scales on plywood infested by lice—
this rude infestation is a sign of the sacred,
    hymn of a black calyx in the mouth of heaven. Hold
onto roughened light, antipoles of abject shame and relief
    after you miss a brushfire zone charred by matchbooks
                    dropped by a nine year-old arsonist. Imagine
you're nine
and must cope with *arson* for the rest of your life.
Tussock moths utter apologies, bowing to milkweed
for our negligence, our ingratitude,
unearned gift of survival.

IF EXCHANGING THE GRAVITY OF BODIES FOR LOVE

Say a pear-shaped curve
is a fruit of tidepools
on a littoral coast. Say a heliotrope
of plasma in a star locks us to our orbit
as if bending the forces of ruptured
bodies for love.

Say a paring knife slid days ago, slicing
my finger, one-inch scar nearly impalpable now
due to zinc and neomycin.
Say a miracle occurs in our natural order,
the transformation
of wedding water to wine.

Say the hands of a mother with child
bleed in sympathy with stigmata
on resurrection day.
The stranger asks, can you prove this?
The sage replies, the question is
how did you bear witness?

MIRACULOUS HEMOGRAPHY IN TRIPTYCH

Did she bleed from dying the hard-boiled eggs with red coloring?
No.
Did she bleed from falling in the back garden, near the fig tree?
No.
Did she bleed from breaking her fall on the stairs?
No.

A FULL MOON FED ON ICE-CREAM MACHINE NICKELS

Thistle-shot lunar meadow of air,
yet no thistles or molecular oxygen
exist on the moon
or in this tickling field,
indigency of stratosphere in zero gravity.
As a girl, I said, the moon
is an ice-cream machine fed with nickels.
I added, *the nickels sweeten the cream.*

Why nickels, I wondered as an adult.
Atomic number twenty-eight,
sacred love-object of selenographers, sextant
of olivine basalt to nocturnal moths
with nickel-colored shadows, in flight
no less than the time
it took to utter *fleece.*

God confirms yea or nay to a warrior-prophet,
one whose name meant destroyer or feller of trees.
Yes and yes instead. Nightly dew on fleece or not.
Girlhood tithe, I offer up a smattering of nickels.

ON MIRACULUM, OBJECT OF WONDER

Toxic diaspora of suns,
our bodies float out of alignment to grace,
vulnerable to affliction or disease,
to errors of sequence, level,
or origin.

When a foxing blade of rust
slid from dill butter to defleshed nerve,
God spoke to the wound, *heal.*
Soteriological miracle of salvation, do not forget
regeneration and incorruptibility.

Under a clock, I found a note saying, *no, thank you*.
Hour to write it more valuable than its contents, I mused.
Now is the time.

THE WORLD IS A FEVER OF DELPHINIUM

No, the world is a fever of delirium, never satisfied.
Or silver nectary of larkspur, sister to ranunculus.
More you partake of the former, more hunger verbs
sea-blood and bone for fish-shaped *tayaki* loaves,
Japanese cakes of boiled azuki beans, black sesame.
Rosewater fingerbowls, hand-squared glass spirals
of angelic ladders. Fever. Yet no tree stands aflame
flourishing where a somnambulent man witnesses
the ruin of his progeny with meager returns,
restless dreams of an immigrant engineer
in bilingual syllables.

camberwise
: arms

slender wing
: theory

by hangars
huiying: in Mandarin

echo :
echolalia

FRAGRANT DISTILLERY OF GRIEF

Fragrant distillery of grief as we ride misery to the hem—
we desire longevity while we fear crossing to a new shore,
hatless women in this rush of tanager wings and tribulation,
a flared bias-cut skirt of aurelian gold wavering
under a murmuration of starlings, urns of donated blood
over a coastal mesa, red dulse swirling on hyaline years—
one hundred seventeen years old with weak or delicate eyes,
of the vituperation of the laborious, storm-wracked vineyard,
of generational wisdom lost in each branch of the family tree,
no matter who marries whom, unloved one with the recipe
for a broth of lotus root and sea salt.

NONE AROSE OUT OF RAPINED EFFLUVIA

Alas, none arose out of rapined effluvia
threshed out of the delta, rice winnowed,
poured in hemp sacks, carried to riverboats,
rattled bones of famine in wind-filtered loess
at the toxic, oil-slackened mouth of the delta.
The river asks of the boatmen, *what is fever?*
The boatmen ask of the fever, *what is delirium?*
The fever asks of the river, *what is happiness?*

LILAC CADENCE SHEDDING MIST-LACED WINGS

The swollen river says, *I arose
from my sickbed*. Monsoon of soaked
termite galleries in the southern light
drilled into grain, nasturtium curling,
triad of seaweed and belly to calves
in algal backwaters, ulna bone
or a brood of juvenile honeybees
in a pelvic quagmire, clef of mud
in a sarabande of the moon's
amorous phase, lilac cadence
shedding mist-laced wings
on my left wrist
at nightfall. The river
says lilac. I say
lyric not
lilac.

A THOUSAND BRIDAL VEILS IN RAIN-BLOSSOMS

A monsoon says, blithely ignoring hexameter
stanzas of wet moonlight, under the aegis of novelty.
No one is responsible for your happiness but you.
Teach us to count drops of acid rain on xerophytes
on the steppes when century-scale global warming
bellows in the contralto tone of dry cisterns, lichen
by the aqueduct: scapular burl of gum eucalyptus,
furze of light on a piazza, inflorescent manzanita
of a thousand rosettes in veils, of rain-blossoms
fashioned by no tillage, no human hand—
clock-faces dropping to asphalt.

GENE EXPRESSION OR BEDAZZLED FERTILITY

Teach us to devour a night of lemonade wedding cake
with green-skinned chardonnay, summer insomnia.
Teach us to change our flesh-colored days of youth.
Teach us what our own poets said, the apostle says.
Teach us to say your name when we arise in darkness,
not to rake yesterday's litter in an onslaught of woe.
Whispers the sage to the stranger, why not confess?
Teach us to strip fresh-cut branches of alba poplar,
almond, or plane trees, then soak them in troughs
where herds come to drink, the future generations
streaked and spotted as figurative grains or stars,
and knowing this action modifies gene expression
or bedazzles fertility hormones in drinking water.

VALIANCE OF GINGER, FRANGIPANI

Light shortens in early winter, a sighing
of ginger, frangipani. Pray for smoky vanilla
girding a wall like barbed wire.

Pray for bees ambling listlessly
after sporadic rains, abdominal temperature
at hiberation levels or end-of-life.

Heat of winter bees, on the contrary,
fails to grow colder in the core of the hive—
flight muscles shiver.

Angels tighten a wing-bolt on a cymbal,
while the bees await
the valiance of ginger, frangipani.

JULIENNED AIR, SNOW UNRAVELS A SLEEVE

Julienned. Our flesh reaps nothing, *nothing*—
forked light in a vapory revolution without verbal
quarantine, without perfume, iodization, radiation.
Saline efflorescence. As a prophet prayed for rain,
a serge-colored cloudbank loosens a sleeve of rain
where waiting is an arduous trial. In a chapel nave,
a room by the sanctuary, lightless without mirrors,
a bride—*not a bird*—by a pendant-bowl chandelier,
drum-linen shades, a credenza of distressed pine.
Keep your wick trimmed, your extra oil on hand.

DELPHINIUM DREAM

Who are you when no one in the room is looking—
Quiet rage of a stranger who asks,
when was the last time you were deliriously happy?

                The sage replies, *what is the evidence of things unseen?*

On prayer as a love-gift of manuka honey
out of a camphoraceous tree
                as a jar of liquid gold poured out of acacia,
                    then black tupelo, *Nyssa sylvatica.*
I hear, *when was the last time you were delphinium?*

                Free-blooming larkspur in the field
            whose folded interior hollers *blue*, petal
                  on petal in the spring.

TAPENADE BATHED IN ORE-FRUITED BLOOD

Rose-quilted silk edged in millimeter cord with tassels,
with macramé butterfly knots, jacketed pupa in a cocoon
a leaf away from the olive grove. Bottle your thirst, salt
tapenade oiled in its own ore-fruited blood. No cardiac
tamponade, a drumming heart. Arrhythmia. Late June,
does a parched olive tree, fruited blood of aquifer gold
nanoparticles say, *I thirst?* How lucid is the yearning
of a honeycomb, drill-tongued nectar
assigned to the task of sating thirst with sweet? *I thirst.*
I thirst. And the new olives sloping to arroyo canyons
and the charred gulleys of brushfire zones. *I thirst.*
No recollection of a stranger asking this question.
And are you salt and light?
Only record is a note I wrote in my teal journal
of pressed star-gazer lilies from a bouquet
after a flight. *Journal d'abord.* A passenger
felt light-headed, and a physician on board
came forward. *How do you feel, ma'am?*
When did you last take your medication?
Jet slowed, descended back to the snowy city.
Silently, I prayed, *dear God. Please heal.* Did not
come forward and offer to pray. Should I have?
Yes. The shame rose like vinegar in the heart,
a lesson too late.

THIS FIELD OF INFLAMED GRIEF, LOOSENED FLAME

Fig and olive crisps toasted in a saltillo oven,
rosemary sticking in the darkest loaves, hairy
parsley roots thinning on a journey to silver,
the bathed spaces of lymph, vinegar sadness
on hyssop—prayer of healing for a uterine bed
of prostoglandin gloss, coral glove in a wet cave
of abdominal aches and odors of rotting scrod
on cotton in a heat wave. Core of red vexation
pulsing on an altar, pulsed by a jellied syrup
of its own fruit, not blood oranges or cacao,
not bitters soaking an ounce of shaved daikon.
Soul, I appreciate your candor. Now please
leave me alone. This will take time. Soul says,
no. Forgive everyone who hurt this temple again
and again in a field of inflamed grief, loosed flame
encircled by a quaking hedge of guardian angels.
Bruised hothouse, this body drizzles a tablespoon
of blood while dreaming up a fabulae of tongues,
an inexorable riptide, a reservoir of verbal waves.

WHY GOD CHANGED THE ITINERARY

God diverted the jet from a catastrophe.
God taught patience to all who would receive.

Isn't God greater than our hearts, asks the sage,
a question mark.

No, I did not ask this stranger who queried me
about the state of happiness as if it were a condition
or a country, not a habit of mind.

Why did the jet return to the airport?
So the souls on board could receive more radiation?
So the airline could avoid a lawsuit?

So the sharks in the ocean could grow thinner?
So God could test our faith? Why not?

ON PULCHRITUDE, ALCHEMY OF GOLD IONS, FURNACED CRIMSON

Prayer as a ducat coin for hand-fired cranberry glass.
Aqua regia, nitrohydrochloric acid, dissolves elemental
gold. Psalm of gold chloride on a bleeding chandelier.
Your net worth is not set by a bridal dowry or price.
Meditate on a field before dawn in a microclime
or a black mountain forest without waterworks—
footpaths in the sight of feral doves or pygmy owls
as witnesses. On pulchritude, crimson alchemy
of gold ions, beauty furnished out of a glory hole—
On praise the color of red plums,
blood of cranberries, of bog-fever.

GOLD FISH, HONEYCOMB OF DELIRIUM

Nuptial air, unspinning lilies of the field
humming, wild doves overhead do not judge
our worthiness of silver or sustenance.
Tongues of fire bless our heads,
kindling languages other than our mother's.

Desire is not a bathetic moonbeam
yearning in the other room, not a ghostly fish
of amorous eccentricities in a lotus pond
languid as a fishtail skirt in the closet,
one I wore last summer.

A gold fish, *honeycomb*. The only fish
bee-cured, then slathered with balm.
Salt-curing, I mean, in the sun.
As for a honeycomb of delirium,
I know of no such fish.

On prayer, I ask you, what bears the light?
Is this happiness? Or the pleasure of fishes
expanding their swim bladders, those fulgent
peonies of isinglass? The necks of icewine
grapes frozen in the vineyards?

SONG OF THE ALBEDO, PSALM OF CORIACEOUS PEEL

Song of the albedo, a psalm of coriaceous peel, our sun.
On prayer as oranges by the mailboxes: a solo *cara cara*
tumbled out of a crate delivered to the back door. Today,
I painted this front door orange for visibility from the sea.
Swarm of miniscules in the hour after sunrise, ionic cloud
of the late winter marina. On prayer at nearly sea level,
not in the high desert where a sun breaks with the deficit
of an exposed lakebed: light fettered by a ginkgo sapling,
terra cotta tiles of the train station, even a dying cockroach
who spent one cold night on its bronze pauldron shoulders
will not last the day. On prayer as honey-milk we drank
as girls after swallowing pills of sulfanomide antibiotics,
sulfa drugs used before pencillin was invented. Glasses
of water would cleanse our kidneys of stones, calculi,
those flinty pebbles of exquisite, razor-edged misery.
Of course, the fog's haphazard monologue, *sotto voce*—
More we say, the more our words cloud our intentions.
Prayer is a tattooed calligram on wayfaring fishermen
arranged in the curve of mooring knots, of lagoons.
God, who is the original verbivore, tetragrammaton
logophile, says to the stranger and sage alike—
rose is a verb.

PRAYER FOR A CAMERAE LYRIC IN THE SEA'S EAR

Lays out possessions with love, not for sale—
Crosses out *for sale* and writes, *everything free.*
Says a prayer for the camerae lyric in a sea's ear,
the chambered spaces inside a nautilus, coiled
like a secret poem yet to be spoken en plein air.
Confesses another language, the idiom of error.
The sea has no ear. A camerae is not a lyric.
Travel mercies for your loved ones, regardless.
Wherever you travel, I go as well, says midnight.
In prayer, I raise you as my blood-daughters.
If you open this chapter, you might hear the sea
withdrawing aromatic seedless flame drupes
red-violet at sunset, recalling the involute joy
of a logarithmic nautilus, introversion
working out its sanctification
in peace.

GOD AND A HYDROPONIC SYSTEM

In this millennium, we say, infrastructure
cloud architect, risk analyst.

God sees us err in the same faults over and over,
our errant pride
without the humility of cirrus.

Anti-didacticism, we resist direct instruction
on ethics, will not circulate in water

or say yes
to yield—

hydroponically speaking, we cannot engineer
a system of common grace on our own,
nor as an act of will,

no more than any of us draws water
by striking a rock in the desert.

God is a hydroponic engineer who aerates lettuce
on aqueous solutions
out of nil.

III.

On Unvanquished Asian Cities

LIST OF UNVANQUISHED ASIAN CITIES

Asian cities are flourishing. Asian cities are vanishing. Asian cities are in quarantine. Asian cities are open. Asian cities reclaim their industrial legacies. Asian cities return to their roots. Asian cities design communal farms with government seed funds. Asian cities generate an excess of light pollution. Asian cities are too dim. Asian cities boast of their seaside night markets. Asian cities fail to offer fishermen modest tax incentives. Asian cities grill fine-boned fish like mackerel, skin on. Asian cities drink the blood of goats. Asian cities sell pangolins and bats. Asian cities import hot goods. Asian cities export cold cash. Asian cities are the *nouveau riche*. Asian cities are ancient empires. Asian cities are filled with eyes. Asian cities are none of the above. Asian cities are beyond the above. Asian cities are unvanquished.

ON HUSBANDRY, NOT HUSBANDS, OR VICE VERSA

On husbandry in this millennium, not animals
especially among city-dwellers. We do not mean
husbanding in an agrarian sense, *per se*.

Those of us commuting by subway or metro
seldom use *husbandry* for the care of crops,
rarely the horticulture of orchids or tea roses—

Under a sky the color of raw goat milk
in this century, we are more apt to say
air quality over *stormy weather*.

Husbandry, nowadays, does not mean
wine-pressing or raising cattle, or fanning
the ox-hide bellows at a forge.

Husbands wandering through the crowds
in a satellite map of Asia, suited or bare-chested,
shout their greetings in a jocular manner.

On husbands of the posthuman, whose husbandry
is beyond the animal, but rather, how husbands
might change the future, morphing.

A SYRAH VINEYARD OF WILD BLACK FRUIT

On a jacaranda-carpeted boulevard of blue-lavender, of azure, *El Niño* rains and ruby-eyed doves swallowed loose gravel, petals, and rice. Rain-kerchiefed women said, day lily, star-gazer, tiger lily dust. We dissolved fragments of stone-ground pity in our mouths, drank the grape-blood of grief in flagons. *Rose from the dead on the third day.* A listless body sown like a grain of seed-wheat into tilled ground. No lighter than a calliope hummingbird en route to a southern winter. Devoured a wheat field broken for us, quaffed a syrah vineyard of fermented black fruit. *I rise. Verb. Rose.* Prayed for a young grandmother, only sixty-one years old, a double-lung transplant. Breathe. *We do this in remembrance of Christ.* Our post-meno-pausal bodies mended of chronic disrepair. Despair, I mean. Never hunger again. *Here is the bread of life.* A body flung asunder like plum flowers torn by ravenous flycatchers, happiness or delirium irrelevant. Prayed for a girl with lymphoma, without medical insurance, without a salary. A spirit of abundance even if not much is there. To the eye. To the solar plexus. To the tongue.

SHAPE OF A BELL OR MIRROR GRACED THE TORSO

Do this in remembrance. Found the rooms clean although I left the bathroom window open. I designated a narrow, second-floor bathroom pane of fogged glass my clerestory, as if I lived in a cathedral. Is it wrong to spiritualize my living spaces overtly, calling an unfurnished nursery a prayer room, et cetera? Set a glass of orange peel, mint, and licorice tea on the nightstand. Opened the ice box, took out a sack of nectarines. How far each orb journeyed on the tips of fruit-pickers to arrive in my mouth, unbruised. How non-georgic, I muse, a child of the millennium, of mushroom clouds, methane, and ancient scripture. Napped in the coolest room with a cross-flow fan spinning. Lemongrass mint. Balsawood. Four o'clock wind gathered shaggy bark under a red gum eucalyptus, redolent debris on the zoysia. *Nothing has belonged to me in the first place. How do we bear the light? As a loaned possession.* When I woke, I rose. Wiped a sill with my sleeve. Smoothness in the shape of a bell or mirror graced the torso of the eucalyptus. *In remembrance.* Put a teaspoon of vinegar on my tongue. Ate the last of the fig, rosemary, and olive crisps glazed in fireweed honey.

BIOENGINEERING A MOSQUITO FASCICLE

Maker of bioinspired needles and mosquito-slim fascicles alike, God dwells in the details of microengineered systems like the biomimesis of syringes. *Toxorhynchitinae.* For what purpose did God invent the mosquito? To draw blood, of course. In a brown-sugar matrix of cassonade, the ant bears a fraction of the colony's winter rations in xylose on its head, shining with cassia oil or the residual heat of the termite mound. Or is it a mythography, out the fish-eye porthole on a whim or a wax seal of autumnal ecstasy. *To wed Christ as your husband. Espoused.* Fire ants and paper wasps feel neither remorse nor gratitude for a cosseted queen whose jarring tenderness is shielded by a drone's short-lived, enamoured noons. Cloud of bees flooding a lion's carcass, their diurnal acts are indivisible from acts of worship. Of gold-footed praise. Or the fallacy of comparing the order of their instinctual labor to the melody of an abecedarian psalm. A bee never ponders anything in the light, but rather, deems it blessed, more divine.

ON FORCES BINDING ATOMS OR BLOSSOMS

Gravity in darkness, not a strong force binding atoms or blossoms, rather, the meek attraction of stars and fish. At dusk, the fisherman, the same one who wheeled out his quadriplegic mother in a flashfire after flyaway sparks from jumper cables ignited the termite-riddled carport, gazes at another silver-haired woman in a yakata kimono, a great aunt snapping her false teeth. Miracle, this senescent aunt, an octogenarian, levitates over the wall at seven in the evening, angel textured with the lean heat of tulip-poplars, strolling to the lake shore swept with a fireplace broom taken from hearthstones still skin-hot. What force of love has sent this image of his aunt from the funeral? What shall he say to his mother, speechless after a stroke? Love.

ECLIPSED BY THIS LINE IN MY GILL

On the vulnerability of gill-bearing life: lungfish, seahorse, an elongated pipefish like a flattened question mark. *So what is our final quest,* sighs a gutted trout on a cutting board, dressed with grassfed butter, chopped dill, and salt. *If I were a mackerel, I suppose at least I could say my name was loaned to the phrase, a mackerel sky.* The first disciples grilled fish on the beach, and at least one was a fisherman, Simon called Peter, with his brother, a duo. Yet thanks to salt seepage and rainless seasons, this evaporating inland sea risks toxic salinization. A shallow body of water of lowering levels says, *hymns of salt and light once resounded in my innards. Swim bladders expanded like giant peonies of isinglass. Liver, fish oil, promises of pearled roe.* Now a knot of angled light floats in this narrowing gallery of fish, a fractured black aquarium.

Finned, I rose out of the water on a hook.
The stranger asked, were you born anew?
The sage replied, why not rise, may I ask?

FIRE-FLOWERS OF PERICARDITIS

The first morning orison
kisses your throat, tunes the red flutes
in your blood. Illumination arises,
a persimmon tree aflame in the hills,
fire-flowers of pericarditis.
On prayer: a myrrh-spiced
wheel of angels, of *Spiritus Sanctus*
stirring a pool as bathers descend
limestone stairs. *Do stairs exist?*
Ordinary bathers ascending,
descending, not angels
with ladders to heaven.

NERVOUS POLYANTHA ROSES MOLTING

Praise the portico by the light of zippered tangelos,
spice cake on a coffee table—molasses, fig spread.
Saying *honeysome* not hunger for a lair of paper moths
devouring a day room of handmade frocks, all cotton.
Of red wine vinegar. Blessed dishes of pears, arugula,
ambrosial lucidity. Jesus ate broiled fish, tree nuts,
dried fig-cakes, olive oil, and wafers made with honey.
Prayer as bellflowers in southern wind, *pétalos de rosa*
on sleek, gun-metal asphalt after the June cloudbursts,
gasoline, bone-fed miniature roses shielded by a cage
yoked with stakes to keep out birds, dogs, strangers.
On a quarter acre of broken polyantha roses molting—
no, shouldering a hedge of turbines, the Holy Spirit.
On the third day, the Son of God rose from the dead
without levitation or a rotorcraft louder than battle,
without metaphorical names of modern helicopters:
sea knight, chinook, firefly, mosquito, angel, zafar.

YOUNG ORCHARD AVENUE

Please do not delay, young fruiting olive
of favor not poverty. *We picked the olives
but never ate them.* Names of streets,
young orchard avenue, though no orchards existed
so far as noons could recall. Olives, a sign of avowal.
Copse of bamboo canes, of prickly pyracantha.
Beauty does not only brace us or hold us still.
I repeat: Flowing not flowering.
In georgics, the fragile vines are high maintenance,
so to speak, requiring a lot of attention.
Olive groves, however, are not.
Sun, wind, rain, sand—the olive flourishes.
Four o'clock, I pray to unravel. Austerity. Pray
to burn the dross in a saguaro-blooming night.
Why should we flower in the dark without eyes—
only the pollen-bearing bats as witnesses,
aria of a rare nocturnal blossom
in the arrows of night constellations,
ravens of blistering rags
after brushfires?

JUNOESQUE

Nonchalance of a stranger who asks,
When was the last time you were deliriously happy?

If a word *zephyr*
lies on the shoulder of a field,
neither love nor virtue
passes the horizon's curve,
or the word, *azimuth.*

Dear God, make us into lightning rods of perfume.

Sequence of stills for a diver—
eagle, double angle, clasp, prayer.

Remember, junoesque
refers to the shapeliness of a slender woman—
not to the blueberry qualities of June
or their post-Juning lateness in this season
after a dry winter.

ZEAL OF COUNTER-CLOCKWISE WISTERIA

Oaxalic red chard. Light not loaned
by the name stirring within,
freely given. Of rugosa, topaz evensong
of bare-root roses for eighty dollars.
Olives, first cold press. Fruits and esters,
a bead of musk on the nose of a rod
in apothecaries or parfumeries, symbiotic
zeal of counter-clockwise wisteria,
a vase of week-old chrysanthemums
with a hungry scent of ethyl acetate,
of pear drops.

NIGHT-BEARING ORCHARDS, VIOLET-TO-GREEN

Praise of pulse-seed, crown gall on your roses,
hybrids of teas and perpetuals, of high noon
fogging a vase of flowering Solomon's seal,
unshaved night-bearing orchards,
violet-to-green plums.

PULSE IN A CAGE OF FIBER-GOLD

On splintering hurricane lamps, a red salvo of iron bullets, a fusillade
of monthly blood, a slashed hachiya persimmon, involute heart-cave
without a pulse in a cage of fiber-gold beaten to aerial filament, angelic
bones, a girl drifting underwater. Sorghum wine flows over a pavilion.
Convolulus vine, thinner than the bars of light fibrillating over koi fish
reflecting an aviary of birds—make room in its lacquered chambers,
dreams of new believers poured out in draughts as moths and silverfish
ascend over clouds of toxic sulfuryl fluoride. Is a terrazzo-floored sea
an illusion of gaiety, of inaudible cantina music after midnight?
asks the stranger. Did I lose a milk tooth in my sleep?
None of the above, says the sage.
Your missing milk tooth
is one of the hundred billion hazy stars in the Milky Way.

KOI, BLOSSOM, PYRIFORM

Aquarium flushed into the lake:
sycamore leaf circled on a pool,
fin of a koi. A fish did not surface
in this body of water. You see?

> Now is the time: this hour
> of an egg-shaped chin will not enlarge any further,
> calyx-end or blossom-end: a cycle finishes.
> You are the pear someone will eat—
> what the living yearn to do.

Semilunar valve of therein, half-moon of regret:
left and right ventricles in a pear-shaped organ. The word is *pyriform.*
On prayer as atria, ears perched on narrow bird-shoulders of the heart,
blue nerves of richest pleasure
in a toxic atlas of self-indulgence.

INELUCTABLE VESSELS OF ATTRACTION

Prayer for the abatement of a flickering retinal migraine, lightning strikes
in one eye with stars and haloes floating at night. On confession exposing
eggplant-colored bruises. *I hated this one, I hated that one.* Not long ago,
the hurts of an aubergine like flags of rage, of outer space irradiating,
spouses who can't stand each other, hating the sacrifice like murder—
for the phrase, *falling in love*, a contradistinction of two bodies enticed
by cups of darjeeling or not, who praise the tang of blood oranges,
and seek those pheromones, the molecules of attraction floating musk
into the air. Our ethos of love is labor, a work of love, no less fragile
than a scrap of lace from a forgotten wedding dress at the thrift shop.

BLUE LOTUS FOLIO

The sage asks, *how do you listen?*
The stranger says, to your body.
God says, do not trust the flesh. *I live in you,*
more than the sum of all luxuries.
If a heart is a chapbook, ten years per quarto
for all quartets of life.
Unfasten yourself at the stitches,
folio on folio.

I was curious about the blue lotus perfume
crushed by hand, depicted in frescoes, plucked
and lifted right to the nostrils. Nurpharine inhaled
for chemically-induced euphoria. Dear Jesus,
is this evidence of things unseen?

The stranger says, why not listen to the world?
So many souls can't be in error, you know.
The sage replies, why don't you ever do
what you already know you ought to do?

JET-BLACK STARS OF HAPPINESS
ON A BOUTIQUE SHELF

Diapason of listening, salt-washed organ
with the stops pulled out, of unseen valves,
clicks, whooshes, and murmurs
exposing radish-colored hurts of the sea,
not far from the blackened jelly of heartache
tangled in kelp, whipped by offshore winds.
On prayer as jet-carbon stars
of happiness on a boutique shelf, of fever
shimmering in the coldest bullet-holes
of a winter night.

ON FLOURISHING HAPPINESS, EUDAIMONIA

To what extent, the dead philosophers wondered,
do virtues of courage, wisdom, or physical beauty
yield flourishing happiness, *eudaimonia* in Greek?
    When I was fourteen, our class toured a basilica
where boys and girls were healed of bone deformities
and left a towering pile of little crutches and leg braces
against the pillars. Miniscule, rose-darkened with age,
cast-off by flesh yet soaked in human anointing oil
mingled with grace. We ate hazelnut chocolate spread
on triangles of toast and strolled north to the basilica.
Tangible awe, my earliest girlhood memory of sensing
the holiness of God outside me. Walking together
for some reason, although we probably rode a shuttle
after ingesting a thousand triangles of giandujia toast—
I did not know, then, that we do live not on bread
alone, but rather, *every word proceeding*
out of the mouth of God.

A QUAGGY BED OF SEAWEED WITH BLOOD-DRUMS

Imagine a stranger, the one
who asks about happiness and delirium
in a tank: hammer-head sharks, cigar sharks,
mako and tiger sharks, juvenile whites.
No stingrays, no barracudas.
Do the sharks ever dwell in bliss or happiness,
or dare we ask, *what is a shark's pleasure?*
What does a shark desire most
in roaming to and fro in the sea?
No dolphins, no humans.
Would you, dear stranger,
dare to ask a shark a question?

True or false: Sharks only deal with intimate violence.
True or false: Sharks never deal with intimate violence.
True or false: A shark is only a cartilaginous cage in the sea.
True or false: A shark does not appreciate unceasing prayer.
True of false: A shark, in its sharkiness, is a squalene stanza.
A shark has no mother or father at home, lying on a quaggy
bed of seaweed with blood-drums pounding in his gills.
The sage asks, *true or false: don't we all lie with sharks*
and live with sharks hidden in ourselves?

ULTRAVIOLENCE

Variation of this episode: the stranger was not an adult.
Rather, a little boy. I listened. Asked to sketch pictures
of the miscreant. Or the stalker, assailant, kidnapper.
Finally, the boy named the sharks, tore up the sketches,
gave me a large paper chrysanthemum. *I do not know*
how to pray, he said. Shredded paper constituted a plea.
Bloodied teeth, prayer of the bones. *Do no harm. Harm.*
I rose in defiance of venom. *Do the little children no harm.*
No. No. Not even ultraviolence. X-rayed toiletries,
patted down by corpulent strangers in nitrile gloves,
a body fortified by tocopherol and monounsaturated fats
out of a dish of avocado-dressed fish I ate on the bay,
ascorbic acid of blood oranges in a honey marmalade,
blood groves—backscatter microrems, weapons.
Do a thousand eyes of bees, in compound sight,
view our pixel-polluted world as sheer ultraviolence—
a permutation or variant of ultraviolet?
The stranger says, you've known me since I was little.
Was your inner whisperer, sowing questions to breed
doubt. I rode the turbid waves of your curiosity at night.
The sage replies, don't you see the souls who turn away
angels unaware, even ones who are little children?
This is one reason why this world is a flown cradle
of lost hearts, of strangers like you.

FRACTURED GROTTO RESILIENCE

Rose. On prayers of buoyancy. Rose. I rose
by a rack of holiday tinsel in a dollar shop,
sea biscuits with dill seeds. Rose-in-a-cloud
garnished with almond slivers. *Do you refer
to the chatoyancy of gems, not their light?*
Fractured grotto of resilience. Swimmer
dives back in a cove. *I rose, yes. Rose.*
Basal rosette scar on my left kneecap.
Cicatrix: a mole nevus, my inner arm
burned with raw cider vinegar, piquant
monosyllabic tones: malt, wine, apple,
odor of rose with rose on rose.

BONE-CORTEX IN A PEONY ROOT FOR MENOPAUSE

Praise for the dank odor of emerald reindeer moss,
pulse of bone-cortex in a peony root as a palliative
for menopause. How many months do I have left?
Black grass jelly cools *qi* with *yin*. Kinship, not shade.
More kin to iodine-black grass, *xian cao* on shaved ice.
This monthly blood which repulsed and drained me
has not depleted my body of goodness.
My heart has a keyhole inlaid with lichen scales
espying the soft moon shadows saying *ember,*
ember, ember while a paraplegic in a night garden
closes her eyes, ghost fires singing *ember, ember,*
while she asks God to touch her spinal cord.
This disease masquerading in my body,
she says, is a stranger within me. My flesh
cannot recognize herself
as herself.

NEVER FALLEN IN LOVE, NEVER FLOWN

Rose this morning and boiled an egg.
Rose. I rose. Free-range, I rose. And rose.

No one heeds me when I testify—
no, never fallen in love. Never flown to Asia minor,
never lived on a boat, never fallen in. Love.
Never. Never. No.

I do not believe you.
I am in denial or what others call
I do not call love.

I call it dystopic love. Dysfunctional love.
A sage might reply,
Why not refer to love without these adjectives?
Love is love on love.

The apostle said, *even if I speak in tongues*
of men and angels...but have not love,
then I am nothing.

There is only the loneliness of a stranger
who inquires about happiness.

FEVER-NOCTURNE OF TACHYCARDIA

Rose is a verb. I rose.
Sagebrush rinsed by a storm,
the moon's cabochons of opal
synthesized in labs,
cardioid roses unfurling.
Swiftly, I strike a sulfur match
on a rooftop of satellite dishes
for data consumption, not actual eating.
Bone-china tea cup of sencha
with a song of crickets in my ear,
folios of book-lungs in air—
the moon is a silicate gemstone
of polyvinal resin tonight.
It is a pot of lentils and rice,
of skins folded into chapbooks,
of borage blossoms and nasturtiums
in neoteric eclogues
gene-edited by agricultural
engineers, new technologies
of crop production.
Aggies, as we say
in our neo-georgic idiom.

GLAZE OF TURPENTINE OR BLACKBERRY HONEY

Seven gallons of fresca on hand-tiled talavera
labyrinthine as the dyed polyester tapestries
woven in a palomino desert. See the foaling
cremello sunrise, rose-colored at the tips?

Gold fur-mantle of a bee. Majolica pottery,
glaze the summer color of blackberry honey—
Only darker than a night's juicy blackberries
is eating those blackberries in organic dark.

AGAVE ROSETTE ON FOREHEADS OR FORELOCKS

Incandescent mesa of planed wind,
agave rosettes on foreheads or forelocks
of wild horses, quake temblors no one notices,
lightning strikes in the Sangre de Cristo,
blood-of-Christ mountains
of citronella beeswax in magnolia-shaped molds,
and the bone-potency of synthetic tiger balm
for mosquito bites on the calves.

Hot oratorio of ginger root, olfactory
in a credenza of ginger candies—not crystallized ginger,
only lozenge bon-bons—out of a tin used for the dollars I earned
by teaching piano to children. *Sweet, it lightens.*
Yes, lightens although it bears almost nothing
in aforesaid light.

FOG CARRIES SEA PERFUME TO YOUR FACE

The downslope fiery winds, Santa Anas—
eucalyptus shedding lime and buff layers,
pollen of genetically modified blue gum,
of mesquite honey, orange blossom
or alfalfa honey not stolen out of hives—
synthesized like illicit butane honey-oil
on the grill, a bonfire of gashed hybrid roses,
petrol-infused coals fueling the mesquite—
Is this mist or a photochemical smog?
*Put to death, therefore, the pleasures
of the flesh*, says the apostle.
Not verbatim in the holy scriptures,
only a gist. More or less. Wander in a tule fog,
streaked hybrid tea roses not at all wild
by a firepit on the marina: fog carries
sea perfume to your face.
This action lightens your mood.

A RUSSET THESIS OF HUNGER

What is so spiritual about fasting? echoes
the pastor. Try it, and I think you'll find out.
On happiness as absence, our nonattendance
as bliss or a unit of hunger. How to measure?
Drachms, gills, clouds of ghrelin and leptin?
Neuropeptide fog triggering hunger pangs?
Arising in a space of apples dubbed honey,
braeburn, gala, fuji, wolf river, or cameo,
a russet thesis of hunger, the hot loaves
of bread melting to glucose in the blood—
brioche, pampano, wolverine, berry, coffee,
cream crullers, babka, tea cakes, naan or roti,
rose-petal drop scones with roasted pistachios,
tangzhong water roux of Taipei, milk Hokkaido
of the Northern sea circuit, loaves of taro-root.
Clarity of heart, increased sensitivity not only
to insulin but matters of the soul, says the sage.
Yet who in the world can stop eating bread?
asks the stranger. Why not change the stones?

LIST OF UNVANQUISHED ASIAN CITIES, A SEQUEL

Asian cities are in the news. Asian cities are invisible. Asian cities are not. Asian cities are locked down. Asian cities are flowering in the recession. Asian cities are deflowering. Asian cities are lowering their taxes. Asian cities are raising their tariffs. Asian cities are rife with the plague. Asian cities have beautiful rivers. Asian cities are polluted. Asian cities are clean and spotless. Asian cities have too much traffic. Asian airports are good for layovers. Asian airports provide lots of kiosks. Asian airports have too much traffic. Flights to Asian cities are on time. Flights to Asian cities are delayed. Only flights over the Java Sea are late. Only one flight. One city. One missing flight.

1. Yangon. *Landed.*
2. Phuket. *Landed.*
3. Guangzhou. *Landed.*
4. Bangkok. *Landed.*

5. Penang. *Landed.*
6. Krabi. *Landed.*
7. Hong Kong. *Landed.*
8. Taipei. *Landed.*
9. Surabaya. *Go to the flight counter.*

The stranger asks, what in the world just elapsed?
The sage says, why does a jet drift outside its flight path?

A WAVE IN MY APPLE MURMURS

One day, I will send a flock of invitations to sages
and fruit-sellers in San Diego, Jakarta, or Mumbai.
There I shall swim, as divers do, with a headlamp
on my forehead, breaking the surface with my face,
by a pod of dolphins grazing a sleek kelp forest's
flexing torque of caress, a mini-glade of strangers.

A wave in my apple murmurs, *not here, take a right*—
a flea market in the cul-de-sac, frothing with dahlias,
anthuriums, roses, and lilies. Why not wrap a dozen
in paper? Late sunlight blesses the skins of mangoes
rolled in cayenne pepper, sold in wax pretzel bags
in fruit-stands by the gutter, so I reach for those.

Fire-blighted apple says, please do not idealize
the rural life, either. Our lost city of angels
barricades a street where the last bookstore
in the world opens its bronze *art deco* doors
to an echolalia of glad voices shouting over
biodegradable honey straws and grapes.

Tough tenderness of those callused mango slices,
fingers of a harpist stroking those bands of light.
I will recover your shattered fuselage of dreams.
If healing comes to you, magnify God.
If you do not seek healing, magnify God.
Even if healing eludes you, magnify God.

IV.

On a Biomythography of Vanishing Bees

STEELED AGAINST FRUIT-BEARING

Pray for the girl who arose from a sickbed
aflame, ravenous for pan-de-maiz
in little yellow cakes
the size of her hand, no larger
than brown-eyed susans in the yard,
rudbeckia triloba, not trilobites,
athropods of extinction.
Hungry, she says to the blasting sun of time.
Blue cornmeal is the color of fossils,
the ancient rocks of ages.
Turn these stones into bread? Nope,
even if this is only a sign
of delirium. Of sunstroke, of famine.
Bread, on the contrary, are stones
we can no longer eat in this millennium.
Allegory, says the stranger.
Unadulterated reality, says the sage.
Hunger is a tribe of denizens
steeled against fruit-bearing satiety.
Do not overlook the desire of an unblossomed fig.
Wrecked, cuffed, imprisoned,
flesh-petaled by scourgings, rose-coiled
innards notwithstanding. Why so close
to love yet beaten out of everything
beautiful yet bare, asks the sage.

ALTERED SHADOW OF AN AIRPLANE OVER THE SEA

A moth-and-rust world of stockpiled possessions, nothing
surrendered. Is this happiness?

On the halfway mark of your longevity predicted
by a wellness algorithm, you look ahead to fewer years lived.

The stranger quotes, no one knows the day or hour.
The sage asks, do you know even the sum of your days?

Passing the altered shadow of a plane gliding on the sea
as it approaches the coast, a gull or dove.

Do you believe God holds a missing flight to the east
in the bright palm of eternity, so to speak?

MARITIME FORCES, SALINE AND ECONOMIC DURESS

What is at stake in all this, I ask. In my fourth decade of life,
I wrote twelve questions on giving, returning, holding or not,
dispatched into a corner of the world. Asked to write postcards
addressed to one another. Vowed to send the cards in a year,
if not a month or less. Did so, as written, stamped to do good.
Strangers mailed valentines to one another, dear ones.

Our bone worlds frozen in capsules as a gift of time—
We relate to our future selves as though we are strangers.
Prayer in a field of milkweed, one pod in a million, freeing
silk-haired astronauts of the air, blended archives of genes,
of capsules split open, seed-vessels. Dear ones, do good—
this is all we can offer in our suits of clay and water.

Deliver questions about a saltillo tile oven
in a lighthouse perched on rock garlanded
with *guano* treacle of gulls: adamantine spar,
dreck of maritime saline and economic duress
in a mercurial sea tainted by disinformation,
not even useful for shaping birds in terra cotta
molded by lowly human hands.

DAUGHTERLY SALT OF THE WORLD

This minute could sing of another life,
yet I am living this one, a day at a time.
Never interrogated strangers on happiness
or delirium. On the contrary, I was queried.
Say if our Messiah were a woman,
female lamb of God, the daughter
risen. How she would arise bleeding
at the ripe age of thirty-three, walking on water
while faint with anemia, rust of iron-sharpening-iron
in discipleship. Feminine light of the world,
shaking dust off her toes. Salt and light,
what would she earn for a living?
Would she learn woodworking from her father?
Would she cast nets with briny fishermen,
a blue-fringed prayer shawl on her shoulders?
Would the daughter of God
collect wisdom's proverbial rubies?
What would she say to future generations
on their red-eye, midnight flights
at the risk of mass vanishings
in a post-religious age,
post-rapture?

LOVE INCARNATE FLAYED OPEN FOR INHERITORS

Promise born of a woman. Mission, *Anno Domini*.
Would female disciples have wiped her ankles with hair
perfumed by a year's wages? Divine matronymic lamb
dying for the sins of the world, bleeding on God's cloth,
olive wood, iron-punctured while onlookers say nothing,
glance the other way, abandon the hour, or outright mock
the mission, souls double-yoked to love beyond the abyss
before modern existentialism took root as a movement.
Crucifixion was the cruelest way to execute a criminal—
Not decapitation, impalement, live burial, or drowning,
not the guillotine, lethal injection, or the electric chair—
rather, divine love incarnate flayed open.

ON PRAYER, A FISH ROLLING IN THE SEA

Three days, three nights. No eidetic visions of porphyry ore, scissors in flight, swallows, or rock doves purling on the cliffs, no mining of aventurine flecked with copper, a blessing to glass-blowers thanks to the expansion of liquid copper at the same rate as hot glass. No butterflies laced with toxic glycoside evoking tawny notes of honey-dust. No lionesses bristling in the hips. No thousand-year old olive groves in sand-swept clay. No viridian sphere of rain, no jute net of fishes, no girlhood juvenilia of minnow-creeks.

The sage asks for a measure of immunity to grant to our ailing bees.

More light than moon shadow in the left eye. No angels or flashing sword-light, rather, the body accepts stem cells or tissue not regenerated autonomously for healing, oblivious to the fruit bats wilting with ragged wings in a cave where hunger pours its own candles and grow cold-sprouted clover and radish. My kingdom for a plum. A pear. An apricot. For now, a miracle of origin: rose is a verb, dissolving blindness in waves of melismatic light, one syllable—

on prayer, a fish rolling in the sea.

IODINE SEAWATER IN A VIAL

On transient blindness. Flying in the dark without aviator glasses, for instance. Or blind spots after staring at contrails in a bright sky, the cotton flavor of nothingness. I tell God about rambutan on the floating markets, the black-fruit syrah vineyards in rhymed signatures, or a gill of iodine seawater in a vial mixed with a turtle's tears, clear as rice vinegar. Shining as the eyes of a girl tasting a slice of angelica wine-cake dark as an iron-fortified tonic in cola. I tell God about starry grit in a pot of honey marmalade, shimmering air of dead pipevine butterflies on a freeway overpass. I tell God not only about sickly bees—also of flying rivers vanishing over Amazonia, of noxious silt under the wings of dying swallowtail butterflies where a widow lives out her dreams at night. Of the bravery of yellow alfalfa butterflies in migration. I say to God, what of anthrax. Say—

Are you in favor of war in this millennium?
Are you an engineer of war or peace?

I tell God about the emerald-green lungs of the world, dying. I tell God about forty-seven girls missing from their village after mudslides. I tell God about scorched chaparral on the fire-blasted coast, and the old paradox of ants—I cannot even recall the paradox in the tale of ants bearing far more than their own body weight on their heads. Or else the perishing honeybees. How a bee-eater preys not only upon bees but also fig beetles and moths in flight. *Did you say the word prey, as in predator, or pray, as in prayer warrior?* I tell God about undersea tureens holding blue-fruiting desires in clandestine slices the color of hope. I tell God about the stolen children of bees, who lose not only their wings but also their instinct for home and family, for honey-making together. I tell God, who knows. All. *Selah.*

BLOUSES OF ASH, IGNITED REAMS OF DATA

You do not believe in reincarnation, but rather, this life only. And behold, you are a bird in this life, no other. In your last days as a seabird over the longest island in the world, you fly to the site where skyscrapers made footprints a long time ago. Now it's floodlights. Look up. A flock of gulls. Mirrored, a window-cleaner washes the eyes of the world with a loofah.

As told by lore, this man—drawn by gravity,
tunneling wind forces, a verticality of air
against the side of the building, fell—
angel of the millennium.

Falling. In his null dreams of surviving the towers. *Falling.* Dress shirts of ash, blouses of ash. Ignited reams of data, a field of black poppies in mid-air: water into firestorm into wind, eye of the hurricane, in motion yet motionless. You are a bird of dreamland, so none of this holds significance. You look in the water for fish or kelp, and seeing none, fly on in sightless gloom.

MARGIN OF AN AZURE DIARY

While sitting in milky bathwater up to my knees, I tell God about the effects of genetically modified pollen on the natural selection of flora and fauna. I say, we are gene-editing for disease resistance nowadays, yet we cannot edit out genocide. What is the correlation of happiness to delirium, fever-ecstasy, or bliss on this flawed journey of flourishing mutagenesis on one hand, and gene therapy on the other? Opening to the gospels and pressing my forehead to the pages, I cool my face on giant print in a language of vanishing bees. Ancient, in other words. Dying bees in the gold-ringed, roseate fingerpads of the divine.

Why not, asks the sage. Do not lose sight of love for a momentary lapse in around-the-clock prayers for the bees. Do see how tongue-speaking prayer warriors operate in a divine engine of light. No plate of tea cakes. No glass of angelica under a black cherry moon. No dollars to trade for beeswax embossed postcards from a loved one to a beloved, with postage lighter than the skin of a redwing peach. On praise as habitude alone rather than what it yields or puts on a table: papaya, daikon radish, scallions, quinoa with radish seeds.

In the end, do the stranger and the sage
ask the same questions?
Why? asks the stranger.
Why not? asks the sage.
Why? Why?

FEVER, VERTIGO, OR NONE OF THE ABOVE

By a chrysanthemum stall, I scribble a to-do list that modulates into mu-
sical notations for flageolets. Months later, there is no trace of a stranger
posing this question, only a note graced by a question mark: *When was
the last time you were deliriously happy?* Fever. Vertigo. None of the above.
Gold and black in the weather-wracked hive of my head, a no-man's zone
of raw honey bleeding with toxicity. Bees do not laugh, not even in the
georgics, at cosmic irony.

Names of clouds—cirrus, cumulonimbus, lenticular, altostratus—subli-
mation of bliss to a trace. Cirrocumulus. Stratocumulus. Nimbostratus.
Anvil. I say, likewise for pondering happiness, i.e. whether flourishing
bees embody or project ebullience, delirium, abundance, or *eudaimonia*.
Flourishing. A fleet of arrows. Transience. The bees, in fact, are oblivious
to spice-drenched attraction, self-actualization, or revitalizing the com-
mon good in a matrix of sweetness mingled with the benzene rings of
indigo dye from a closed factory.

Bees do not experience states of happiness
like human beings, our nuclei palaces of delirium
oozing with dopamine.

NAPES OF CREPUSCULAR GOLD

Yield of sister ice-blossoms and apiarian transparency, double-edged nectar of strife. *Here is what I can reconstruct out of lost-poem fragments—translated into prose.* When the daybook is closed, a coastal mesa does not heed the darkness of forty-kilo stones. An angel of the millennium plunges over green valleys, calla lilies with napes of crepuscular gold pouring bridal glory on chaparral trails to the sea.

While the angel navigates the hierophantic, negotiating the visible and invisible, parasailers glide like Icarus on wax wings in hot air balloons and zeppelins invented only a century ago.

Is this a dead metaphor? The world is igneous rock while orange-yellow squash blossoms are spoken by God out of the ground. A centenarian plucks the blossoms to garnish the darkest dark chocolate ganache. She never married, smoked, or drank to excess. Out of oyster-rich, mossy skin, in the gold-black cadenza of her days, this woman blesses an astro-silk seed—*taraxacum*—a floating stroke of kindness out of milkweed—*do no harm* out of a century of prolonged civil wars, epidemics, fruit-bat fever. No harm. Harm.

NO REASON FOR MODIFIED ORANGES

In an agrarian paradise, oranges would kiss fire, not blight,
not go into oblivion. In this life, the converse is true. Groves
may no longer exist one day, no reason for modified oranges
to touch the ground at all. Orchards already no longer exist.
No reason for navel-only, seedless, frost-resistant oranges.
No yellow oranges. *Oroblancos.* No grapefruit or pomelos
aloft in space. Blowing veils across a waterfall whose ledge
you fail to see, whose age is neither colonial nor decolonial,
a holy cloud blessing the upper clerestories of grace.
Full moon shimmies in chiffon bought with twenty nickels.
You never dove like a swan, never plummeted over falls:
you bungeed gleefully across a gorge—
In hindsight, you recall those wistful stanzas of azure:
summer girlhood lessons: floating on your back, torso
aligned to a chlorine tranche of waves, scripts of bones:
never jumped off a ledge, olive-skinned: you never sank,
never swam by the jetty in a lake. Rather, a disavowal
of what was there: no fear of drowning, a swan not:
yet God held you on a wing while you kicked:
Why does happiness matter? Or delirium? Ask instead,
what bears the light?

SHAKUHACHI, KHLOY, PAIXIAO, DANSO

In the rain, a stranger whistles
Greensleeves on a polyvinyl
panflute of water pipes.
Plumb a restroom with these,
melodious as four bamboo flutes:
shakuhachi, khloy, paixiao, danso.

What we fail to say lies in a fossil burrow
of permafrost. As I listen to God,
as if we spoke about this before, our prayer
is a thirty-thousand year-old campion blossom
frozen prior the end of the Ice Age.

God says, the bees, the bees.
The sage says, love
is a four-wing saltbush in the desert,
a time capsule.
God is love, say the bees.

Says the stranger, I've never fallen in love.

A campion bud is pristine
as if it arose out of the permafrost
of its own volition. Or the delirium
of revival, of happiness.

AGE OF MICROPROPAGATION

What millennial bee will find this bud
rolled on a petri-dish?
In this age of micropropagation, eons
after the epoch when a campion blossom
froze in a cryotic burrow of soil,
propagating cells on the micro-level
does not effectively multiply
our sense of intimacy or diminish
our isolation, every soul in an igloo
inside an igloo.

CIRCUMGYRATION OF AN ORBIT AT APHELION

> Circumgyration
> at aphelion, far from the sun.
> Swallow, forked or scissored.
> No, a hairpin saved from falling
> out of spring maidenhair,
> this feathery dome, a delirium
> of tossed stardust, not birds.
> In my fortieth decade,
> in a diphthong of light,
> two wedded vowels—

rising, falling body
at sea level, nothing
of mineral water I drank
in flight, rather, adoration
and calmness like spoons
at twenty thousand feet
ten miles from the coast,
even without a hundred
prophets hidden by God,
fifty and fifty in caves.

BEE-ADORNED, A GLORY-HOLE FURNACE

Spring rain of raspberry-mint lemonade garnished with quartered limes, no more than a teaspoon of salt. A nimbus cloud, full of drops, takes the shape of a pontil scar where a vase broke off a rod. Concave, when you hold the vase upside-down, a pontil scar's curve is enough to hold an egg or your elbow. Yesterday, I did not possess anything other than my own skin, the largest organ of the body, and maybe not even the skin on my back, as the saying goes. Now in hand, I balance a tumbler of aromatic rain and brandywine raspberries on my walk to the lake where I spotted the koi emulate a drowning leaf under the birch catkins shedding nut-brown tears.

In my fortieth year, I broke one of my own rules.
Never throw away a poem. Good housekeeping—
my excuse to no one in a bee-adorned vision,
a blazing glory-hole of its own making
where the molten
curls like a liquid flower
in a furnace, grows afire.

SOLO FLOWER VASES, FIRE-POLISHED

Fumigated, singed on a lathe of fire, carbonized to their vanquishing: at least forty, if not a hundred lost poems, not their fault. Forty or fifty, if not more, or as a multifoliate thousand flowers, millefiori beads around solo flower vases, fire-polished, lead-free, ridged and knurled in vaults to cool without stress. Fragile chromosomal breakage of our soul-flowers in a fleshy portmanteau, *soliflore*.

> What if they belonged to a *soliflore*
> of floral lilies outlined in sepia ink, no longer
> than a page, denied a right to a voice
> or a vote?

THIRTY-TWO THOUSAND YEAR-OLD CAMPION

Frozen cells of a thirty-two thousand year-old campion flower excavated from tundra permafrost, cloned and micropropagated in vitro. The isolated fruit tissue is *placental*. No floral poverty in blood jars, not in our void granaries of famine.

What shipwreck or cave must I explore, what speleology
to retrieve the lost ones?

GLASS OF LEXICAL DENSITY, VANISHING BEES

If I waited another year, flitting out of sight
with mute opalescence, not zirconia-crusted
melodrama, would I infer the replies
to their queries? How do we speak of the lost—
a missing generation or never extant?

> No door, their stanzas will never see
> topoi of darkness, of lexical density
> pulsing at a rate slower than our blood,
> shattering rather than flowing
> like centuries-old window glass—
> denser at the foot of each pane,
> motion of centuries touching us,
> a stillness of a rose in a rose
> akin to a silence of bees.

Even if you used one of those telescopes
or infrared binoculars at night, you would not see the lost
tethered by silver-sleeved night, nor X-ray films
of wisdom teeth budding in the bone.

A COMET CANNOT HOLD AN ATMOSPHERE TO ITS OWN BODY

Over Siding Spring, an obscure body flies by this globe
on a close pass in a wilderness of creosote and firestorms,
telescopes in an observatory of ash, dishes of *xiaolongbao,*
garden of chives tended in a biodome, while the Oort Cloud
births frozen comets of irradiated pumice, solid methane:
a comet is way too small to hug an atmosphere to its bones,
not enough gravity to anchor spiracles of lost gas
on a flyby once in a blue moon, so to speak,
while the naked eye of a star-gazer
glimpses a blurred tail
a thousand meters above sea level.

ROUGH BONE-MARL AND FRUITAGE OF THE SEA

On sadness as a winged, maple samara spinning to the grass. I lost the word, zephyr, to the wind. This tree of my girlhood surrendered millions of its green children. Zero-sum. Silt-blackened book lying on the tickling shoulder of a field which the sage says is seen by a red-shouldered hawk in flight. A hairnet in a sea wreck of fuselage is visible to the God of the universe even after the plane, a neon blink, vanishes from the flight radar.

On a macadam road to weekly flute lessons, my bicycle wheel slid into a rut. Out of my basket, four books of arpeggio exercises and chromatic études dropped into the gutter. No gill of juice siphoned from kelp's chlorophyll tresses, no fish bones boiled to gelatin to seal the slash—rough bone-marl and azure fruitage of the sea—gauzeless yet not guile-less, I put my ungloved finger in a wound.

Out of the wound arose a verb. Rose.

REFUSAL OF POST-LYRIC FRAGMENTS

Out of a dossier of loose stanzas, those lost poems—interleafed, engulfed petals—tossed in the duration of a year. A bleak refusal of post-lyric fragments. Anti-roses.

Why? I could not envision how the lines would progress beyond their fledgling syllables, wings of nihilism hanging upside down in a tree.

Why not? I failed to coax them into palindromes, mirror-hinges refusing to fuse. In either state of being, regardless, happiness or delirium, I offered nothing.

What about skin-grafting onto a dish of agar and incubated *in vitro*? The gaze of changeling poems—asterisks of faded concerns, terra cotta doves in hand, never in flight—

Would the little poems survive?
Fear not, little ones, the flocking of raucous anxiety like crows into the fox-eyed moon.

Fear not, dear grasshopper. *Selah.*

BUGONIA, NOT BEGONIA

A furred gold-black drone, solo laborer, dozed on the seed-head of a poppy. The drone was away from the hive, exiled to a lair of dandelion fur over here, a poppy head over there. Did a footloose brood vanish like myrrh smoke on a peppertree lane? Did electromagnetic fields or nuclear radiation drain their vitality? Is our disaccharide nectar toxic—factory-bottled blue agave, dyed fructose colas? *Blue agave is not always blue,* says the sage. *Bugonia,* not begonia, mythical regeneration of bees.

Bugonia, not begonia. Names are not the thing itself. Virgil said new bees spontaneously arose out of a carcass treated with mud, wattles, and thyme. A wax palace of hexameter: Honey-dressed ox or lion carcass larded with clay, a thousand bees roaring like coins minted in a furnace. *Apis mellifera,* oriency of the dewlap fold loaned to unmanned aerial vehicles, spiracles of air. Not so much bodily happiness, not even a state of recklessness in the loosened bliss of biomythography.

WINTER NIGHT ASKS FOR A FLOODLIGHT

The sage disrupts my dialogue
with the winter night, asking—
Would you please bring me a floodlight?
How am I to go out into the world
without a light? Would you please?
How shall I find the lost if you refuse?
A filament burns out, short
shelf-lives of light-emitting diodes.
You must find this floodlight for me.
I was not going into the world to find it.
Titanium or tungsten filament. Halogen.
Iodine or bromide. Fluorescent. Please?
Could be the one right above my door.
No, it is burning out.
No other floodlight than the one you see.
Hold on, then. Shall we go,
together, into the darkness,
where our voices stay the light—
dabs of voluptuous honey,
of common grace?

FIG-EATING BEETLE SIZE OF A SILVER DENARIUS

Epaulettes of a dying fig-eating beetle size of an ancient silver denarius
not lasting the night—a fig-eating beetle, not the denarius—in a spray of
starlight. Rolled cotton scrim, seven stories up. Attention distilled from
patience. Go to the right, shadowed by the proverbial crucifix, a fig tree
no one sees, an ant's powerful mandibles carrying a grain of coconut
sugar, an oared rowboat seeking lost ones, of inland wind breaking over
the lake, dashing sand in the mist—yet soundless on the dunes, miles
away. I bear right—

no one is there, only
redwoods, the ginkgos
underfoot, fruit-pods
open to expose bitter
urushiol on a lint cloth,
ailanthus *tree of heaven*
weeping an odor
of exhausted
young mothers
on naproxen.

BLACK AQUARIUMS LOVE VOTIVES

Milk-and-iron odor of rain
on macadam. Fig-eating beetle does not revive
as though lying intestate, the sum of its assets—
a maidenhair ginkgo, an unleashed willow—
what else does a dying fig-eating beetle own?
The armor shielding its moonstruck back,
a gleaming bouquet of camellia
and ranunculus in its eye?
What can a fig-eating beetle muster in peace,
what salary-in-salt, what love-offering
of silk-spinning moths
and shadflies with only hours in the day?
One flaring orchid, cattleya sepal
cooler than dollars on human skin,
tulip-streaked virus, full or light-breaking?
X-rayed chrysanthemums in a cyanotype
of black aquariums, of votives
at the very instant the wax melts—
to flow without burning,
to flower without delirium
or ecstasy.

A FLOATING RIVER-MARKET OF THE UNDERWORLD

Wayward seabirds, a murmuration of cape starlings,
pulp of mangosteen fruit in a floating market,
neither bone nor coral. June heart, a fist or rope.

Prayer scales a barnacle-blossomed shelf
like memory beyond forgetting in the first place—
a stranger asked the question, *when was the last time
you were deliriously happy?* Who could recall?
Could I? *Can you forgive me?*

Fever could be delirium, but not happiness.
Dearth of oxygen. *Delirium.* Or happiness
is not always fixed at the level of delirium.

Holding a child without desiring one of my own
is happiness without delirium. Was my name,
in the first millennium, thespian? Do I recall
my beloved's glance before dark hadean mists
hastened my final return to the underworld?

Here, do I have peace beyond understanding,
or do I harbor the secret of contentment in all
contexts, even one as abhorrent as this? No.

XENOPHOBIA OR VELVET LABOR

A lyre, translated into stars,
hangs in the sky. Lyra,
the brightest star inside it, Vega.

Lost poems, thanks to memory, flew back
to this life. I shall never regret
this fleeting moment of letters opened
when velvet labor, unspinning
like lilies, switched to praise.

At what moment in time
does xenophobia cross the threshold
to love, not strangeness?

PRAYER FOR A STRANGER

Open a stone door by the name of Jesus.
The word, *sphragis*, for a wax seal. Figuratively,
closing a poem. Sphragis, not sphagnum moss.
Could not even recall a face or name, yet an invocation arose.
The world, turning from night to sunrise: I rose.
And may they be in us so that the world
will believe you sent me.
On happiness and delirium. Rose is a verb.
A blind woman opens her eyes: I rose.
A girl with cancer of the cervix says: I rose.
This battered work of scribes: rose.
A song in the nightjar's slit throat: rose.
Redemption in an expanding universe—
Who, after lying in a tomb for three nights, rose?
Rose.

V.

Epilogue: An Echolalia
of the Unadorned

AN ECHOLALIA OF THE UNADORNED

Do not shun firelight—Happiness is not an end,
a system, or a method. Rather, love
unconditionally.
Hold onto ones who love, and those who do not—
Hold everyone you love
loosely, my dear.
Please listen.
Do not overlook the potential of an unblossomed fig.
For now, it is a miracle of origin—
—*Selah.*

NOTES

The genesis of *Rose is a Verb: Neo-Georgics* consisted of notes on twelve questions I designed as poetry exercises for a class I taught at the Glen Workshop in Santa Fe, New Mexico, sponsored by *Image: Art, Faith, Mystery*. The notes gradually developed into micro-essays which morphed into poems—some of the original micro-essays appear in the second half of the book.

With its cyclical nature imagery and motifs concerning happiness, I noticed parallels to Virgil's *Georgics*. Subsequently, I studied four translations of the *Georgics*—two online texts (one translation in poetic stanzas, the other in prose), plus two print bilingual translations—intrigued by similarities between the Mediterranean setting in the *Georgics* and southern California, where I resided at the time: olive groves, vineyards, the life of bees, agronomic sciences, catalogues of trees, soil chemistries, the sea coast, and unfortunately, the brushfires, to list some examples.

Reading further, I researched literary criticism on the *Georgics* and contemplated the various historical events that elapsed since Virgil wrote the *Georgics,* circa 29 BC—the crucifixion of Christ, advancements in agricultural technology and genetic engineering, nuclear warfare, the digital age, the axial precession of our earth's rotational axis (influencing which star constellations we see in the sky), transportation (airplanes, trains, and cars vs. chariots, for instance) and vanishing bees—in contrast to the didactic tone of Virgil's long poem infused with lessons, political allusions, omens, and over two thousand verses in Latin hexameter. However, despite the inevitable changes over time, many social and environmental dangers persist to this day, including brushfires, war, pandemics or epidemics, and anthrax, whose infectious symptoms are detailed in Book III.

The four parts of my book echo the progression of Virgil's the *Georgics*: Book I—agrarian labor like tilling the soil, weather signs, and war omens; Book II on olive groves vs. vineyards ("The Vituperation of the

Vines"), birth of trees; Book III on animal husbandry (i.e., veterinary care, procreation), cycles of life in nature; and finally, Book IV, a "bio-mythography" of bees. I also explore Virgil's Epicurean-influenced questions in the *Georgics*: What is the ultimate path to happiness? What is pleasure? What is a good life? And so forth.

Exemplary poems and excerpts by Jimmy Santiago Baca, Mei-mei Berssenbrugge, Rita Dove, Jane Kenyon, Rolf Jacobsen, Denise Levertov, Czesław Milosz, Wisława Symborska, Arthur Sze, Afaa Michael Weaver, a Pueblo Indian Prayer, and a passage by Søren Kierkegaard were considered and discussed alongside each attendee's original work at the arts festival.

The epigraphs on the *Georgics* are excerpted from the *Oxford Dictionaries Online* and *Oxford Classical Dictionary* edited by Simon Hornblower, Antony Spawforth, Esther Eidinow. New York: Oxford University Press, 2012. The quotation ("The time for harvest") is excerpted from the first section of *The Georgics* by Virgil, translated by David Ferry.

~

Part I

Information about cloud-seeding with rockets of silver-iodide: "Will We Ever…Control the Weather?" by Colin Barras. *BBC News: Future.* 5 May 2014.

"Life is more than food, / and the body more than raiment." Paraphrases Luke 12:23.

"God is greater than our hearts." New International Version, 1 John 3:20.

"If I abandon my body to flames, yet have not love, / I am nothing." Paraphrases 1 Corinthians 13:1.

"Put to death, therefore, the pleasures of the flesh." Paraphrases Colossians 3:5.

From *Walden* by Henry David Thoreau: "The mass of men lead lives of quiet desperation" is paraphrased in the line, "Most of us may live in quiet desperation."

Part II

The list of trees is quoted from the second section of Virgil's *Georgics*.

"every word proceeding / from the mouth of God." Paraphrased Matthew 4:4.

"if we praise happiness as justice, but rather, deem it blessed: as something more divine and better." Paraphrased from Book I.12 of the *Nicomachean Ethics* by Aristotle.

Silence is a 1966 novel by the Japanese writer, Shusaku Endo.

Part III

Book III of Virgil's *The Georgics* alludes to "vanquished Asian cities." Conversely, the line in my poem refers to "unvanquished Asian cities."

The list of "unvanquished Asian cities" is excerpted from a flight screen for a missing Asia Air Flight which departed from Surabaya, Indonesia, for Singapore on December 28, 2014.

"Faith is the substance of things hoped for / the evidence of things unseen." New King James, Hebrews 11:1.

On flying rivers over the Amazon rainforests, please refer to Brazilian climate scientist Professor Antonio Nobre's research in "The Flying Rivers Phenomenon."

Part IV

The clonal micropropagation of a Siberian campion flower is described in the article, "Dead for 32,000 Years, an Arctic Plant Is Revived" by Nicholas Wade. *New York Times*. 20 February 2012.

The Mars flyby of Comet Siding Spring is reported in *Sky and Telescope*, "Spacecraft Observe Comet Siding Spring" by Kelly Beatty. 23 October 2014.

"Bugonia" refers to the bio-mythological regeneration of bees from an ox carcass, as mentioned in Book IV of the *Georgics*. Incidentally, this phenomenon also occurs in Judges 14:8-9, when Samson takes honey from a swarm of bees in a lion's carcass.

Information about the vanishing bees: "Vanishing Bees." *Natural Resources Defense Council*. 25 July 2008. As stated in the article, "Researchers call the mass disappearance Colony Collapse Disorder, and they estimate that nearly one-third of all honey bee colonies in the country have vanished."

"as foxes live in holes and birds of the air, their nests..." Paraphrases Matthew 8:20.

"And may they be in us so that the world will believe you sent me." New Living *Translation*, John 17:21.

WORKS CONSULTED

Virgil. *The Georgics.* Project Gutenberg.

Virgil. *The Georgics: A Poem of the Land.* Translated by Kimberly Johnson. New York: Penguin, 2009.

Virgil. *The Georgics of Virgil.* Translated by David Ferry. New York: Farrar, Straus and Giroux, 2005.

Virgil. *The Georgics of Virgil.* Translated by J.W. MacKail, 1934. Internet Sacred Text Archive.

ACKNOWLEDGMENTS

A portion of this book appeared in *Angels Flight: Literary West* in a slightly altered form.

This book was set in Perpetua, designed by the British sculptor, artist, and typographer, Eric Gill, in response to a commission in 1925 from Stanley Morrison, an influential historian of typography and adviser to the Monotype foundry. The design for Perpetua grew out of Gill's experience as a stonecarver and the name pays tribute to the early Christian martyr, Vibia Perpetua.

This book was designed by Shannon Carter, Ian Creeger, and Gregory Wolfe. It was published in hardcover, paperback, and electronic formats by Wipf and Stock Publishers, Eugene, Oregon.

The cover image is *Rose VIII*, by Jim Morphesis, 2011. Oil and mixed media on panel. 26 x 26 inches. Used with permission.

Made in the USA
Coppell, TX
17 September 2021